CAMBRIDGE LIBRARY COLLECTION

Books of enduring scholarly value

Cambridge

The city of Cambridge received its royal charter in 1201, having already been home to Britons, Romans and Anglo-Saxons for many centuries. Cambridge University was founded soon afterwards and celebrates its octocentenary in 2009. This series explores the history and influence of Cambridge as a centre of science, learning, and discovery, its contributions to national and global politics and culture, and its inevitable controversies and scandals.

Bibliotheca Pepysiana

Samuel Pepys (1633-1703) was a student of Magdalene College, Cambridge, and bequeathed his personal library of 3000 volumes to the College on condition that the contents remained intact and unaltered; they remain there, in his original bookcases, to this day. In the early twentieth century, a project to produce a complete catalogue was begun, and four volumes were published between 1914 and 1940. Volume 3 lists 51 volumes of medieval manuscripts, some of them consisting of several items bound together. The author, the outstanding palaeographer and prolific writer of catalogues M.R. James, remarks on the almost total absence of Latin liturgical and theological manuscripts, and calls attention to the historical, literary and scientific writings in English and French, several picture-books, an interesting 'scrap-book' and a unique copy-book from 1400 included in Pepys's collection. This book continues to be a valuable resource for medievalists and Pepys scholars alike.

Cambridge University Press has long been a pioneer in the reissuing of out-of-print titles from its own backlist, producing digital reprints of books that are still sought after by scholars and students but could not be reprinted economically using traditional technology. The Cambridge Library Collection extends this activity to a wider range of books which are still of importance to researchers and professionals, either for the source material they contain, or as landmarks in the history of their academic discipline.

Drawing from the world-renowned collections in the Cambridge University Library, and guided by the advice of experts in each subject area, Cambridge University Press is using state-of-the-art scanning machines in its own Printing House to capture the content of each book selected for inclusion. The files are processed to give a consistently clear, crisp image, and the books finished to the high quality standard for which the Press is recognised around the world. The latest print-on-demand technology ensures that the books will remain available indefinitely, and that orders for single or multiple copies can quickly be supplied.

The Cambridge Library Collection will bring back to life books of enduring scholarly value across a wide range of disciplines in the humanities and social sciences and in science and technology.

Bibliotheca Pepysiana

A Descriptive Catalogue of the Library of Samuel Pepys

VOLUME 3: MEDIEVAL MANUSCRIPTS

MONTAGUE RHODES JAMES

CAMBRIDGE
UNIVERSITY PRESS

CAMBRIDGE UNIVERSITY PRESS

Cambridge New York Melbourne Madrid Cape Town Singapore São Paolo Delhi

Published in the United States of America by Cambridge University Press, New York

www.cambridge.org
Information on this title: www.cambridge.org/9781108002059

© in this compilation Cambridge University Press 2009

This edition first published 1923
This digitally printed version 2009

ISBN 978-1-108-00205-9

BIBLIOTHECA PEPYSIANA

PART III.—MEDIAEVAL MANUSCRIPTS

NOTE

Not more than 500 copies of the complete Catalogue
will be issued ; but owing to the special appeal made by
one or two of the Parts, a limited number of extra copies
of such Parts has been or will be printed for independent
sale.

The Illustrations, consisting of photographic facsimiles
will be issued in a portfolio as a separate Part.

A DESCRIPTIVE CATALOGUE OF THE LIBRARY OF SAMUEL PEPYS

PART III. — MEDIAEVAL MANUSCRIPTS

By Dr. M. R. JAMES

Provost of Eton : sometime Provost of King's College

—

LONDON:

SIDGWICK *&* JACKSON, LTD.

MCMXXIII

[Temporary Title-page.]

MEDIAEVAL MANUSCRIPTS

INTRODUCTION

HE present section of the Pepysian catalogue contains an account of the mediaeval manuscripts and some others of literary interest. In compiling it I have followed the method employed in my other catalogues of manuscripts : the order in which the books are described is simply that of their places on the shelves, an order dictated largely by considerations of size.

The only printed catalogue of the Pepys Manuscripts which professes to give a general view of the collection is that which appears in the Oxford *Catalogi Manuscriptorum Angliae et Hiberniae* (1697 II. 207). It is entitled : Librorum Manuscriptorum viri sapientissimi *Samuelis Pepysii,* Curiae Admiraliae nuper a secretis, varii quidem argumenti, sed praecipue de re navali, quae est Anglorum gloria ac Praesidium, Thesaurus inaestimabilis.

The numbering (a double one)[1] runs from 6716 (1) to 6848 (129), and the catalogue has these subdivisions :

> *Historical*: 6716 (1) to 6730 (15).
> *Political*: 6731 (16) to 6749 (30).
> *Religious*: 6750 (31) to 6766 (47).
> *Mathematical*: 6767 (48) to 6785 (66).
> *Poetical*: 6786 (67) to 6792 (73).
> *Mixt*: 6793 (74) to 6809 (90).
> *Naval*: 6810 (91) to 6848 (129).

(With a sub-heading at 6835 *Of Naval Architecture*, which, however, does not cover all the items that follow it.)

This catalogue, as has been said, was issued in 1697 : it may have been drawn up some years earlier. Pepys did not die till 1703 ; not all his

---

[1] The first numbering is that which runs through the whole volume: the other is that of the single collection.

manuscripts, therefore, need appear in this list. That fact will account for some incompleteness in the catalogue. I have not tried to discover exactly how incomplete it is in other departments; but in my own I find that 14 volumes out of the 51 which I describe are not entered in it.

It has another imperfection, one of method. A single volume, if it contains several treatises, is split up, and a separate entry and number given to each treatise, so that the number of entries is swelled much beyond the number of volumes. The nineteen entries of *Mathematical* books, for example, are comprised in three manuscripts. Thirty-seven volumes described by me have sixty entries in the old catalogue.

Of losses which the collection has suffered in the section with which I am concerned I can only find one to record: 6779 (60) Bernardus Silvester de Virtute ac Essentia Planetarum et Constellationum cum figuris. Pergam.

Of omissions in the present volume—or (as I would rather put it) of volumes and tracts not included—there are many. Taking the old printed catalogue as a basis, I find that of the 15 *Historical* articles I have here described 6; of the 14 *Political*, 3; of the 16 *Religious*, 15; of the 19 *Mathematical*, 18; of the 7 *Poetical*, 5; of the 17 *Mixt*, 11; of the 39 *Naval*, 1. Those which are passed over are all of quite late date, except two, viz. Caxton's translation of Ovid's *Metamorphoses*, printed from the manuscript by George Hibbert in 1819 for the Roxburghe Club; and the Maitland Poems, the entire text of which is being edited for the Scottish Text Society.

On the other hand, I have included, either by request or because they happened to interest me, several manuscripts which are no older than some which I have left out. Two or three volumes, moreover, are common, in virtue of their subject, to the mediaeval and to other sections: they contain music, or naval matter. These I have not attempted to treat from the specialist's standpoint.

As to the composition of the collection. Without doubt the volumes containing English prose and poetry are the most famous. The religious poetry has been included in Professor Carleton Brown's admirable *Register of Middle English Religious Verse*, published by the Bibliographical Society in two volumes, to which I have given references. The Chaucerian pieces

(2006) have been long known. To Poetry I reckon Nos. 1236, 1461, 1584, 1999, 2006, 2011, 2014, 2030, 2101, 2125, 2344. English Prose is an important constituent in 2125 and 2498. There are also medical and other receipts in 878, 1047, 1307, and portions of the Bible in 1576, 1603.

More recent verse is in 1999 and 21 and there is the bulky rhymed Chronicle of Herdinge in 2163.

The most important French books are the Apocalypse (1803), the Vegetius, etc. (1938), and the Guillaume de Machaut (1594). The Coronation of Claude (1791) is an interesting, but ugly book. Jean Mallart's little book (1607) is illustrated with woodcuts.

The ordinary ingredients of a collection of manuscripts are not to be found here. Not a single Latin Bible, Psalter, Missal, or Breviary did Pepys acquire. There is but one book of Hours—but that is interesting from the number of commemorations of Scottish saints which it contains (1576). One patristic manuscript—Isidore (2808)—and that not theological: no Scholastic Divinity, no Canon or Civil Law. The Medical books are English. Science does contribute two, both of some interest, the volume of mathematical treatises (2329) obtained by Dr. Dee (quite honestly) from Peterhouse, and the Bacon (1207) which was also Dee's. Alchemy (1295) follows at the heels of Science, and Magic (1530) on the heels of Alchemy. Among the historical books I reckon 1461, 1791, 1955, 1998, 2014, 2099, 2163, 2191, 2244, 2314, 2516. They are a motley array: some belong to more than one category. I call attention here only one (2314), which must come from St. Augustine's, Canterbury, and, if I mistake not, is closely connected with the better known manuscript of Thomas of Elmham at Trinity Hall. This is almost the only manuscript with a fairly clear monastic provenance.[1] The pretty Kalendar (1662) that was written at Durham, was probably used by a layman.

Coming to the artistic aspect of the books, I unhesitatingly place first the mediaeval sketch-book (1916). There are very few such things anywhere, and I believe that this of Pepys's is the only English one in

---

[1] The word provenance having occurred, I take the occasion to observe that it seems useless to expect any information from Pepys's papers as to when and whence he procured his manuscripts, other than naval. The bill for Spanish books, lately published by Mr. Gaselee in the *Transactions of the Bibliographical Society*, appears to be the only document of the kind which has survived either at Oxford or Cambridge.

existence. Though it is later and less important in many ways than the famous book of Villars de Honnecourt, at Paris, which has been twice at least reproduced in full, it would amply repay a special monograph.

The other notable picture books are the Apocalypse (1803), and the Speculum (2359). Vegetius (1938²) has some fair pictures, the Coronation Claude (1791) some bad ones, the Kalendar (1662) some very nice drawings.

The complete list of picture books is : 1576, 1594, 1662, 1791, 1803, 1916, 1938², 2258, 2359.

The Octateuch (1603) has some very clever late restorations of illumination in it.

Palaeographically the scrap-book (2981) is by far the most interesting. Its specimens of early writing, from the eighth century onwards, include some very great rarities. It would be a good thing if they could be detached so as to render the verso-sides visible ; but so far this has not been found practicable. The last item in my catalogue, a 'copy-book of about 1400' is not impossibly unique. I at least have never seen another.

I am afraid that this catalogue may have suffered a little from the long interval which has of necessity elapsed between the writing of it and its appearance in print. During that time I removed from Cambridge to Eton, and it became no longer possible to refer to the manuscripts themselves, to verify small points, or to resort to libraries, with the same ease, and keep abreast of publications of texts and periodical literature. The catalogue is therefore in essentials a pre-war production. I submit, in palliation of defects which may be found in it (I am thinking principally of references to modern editions) that no catalogue can be absolutely up to date : in fact, one object of the cataloguer is to pave the way for others to supersede his own work by publishing texts and studying pictures and scripts to which he has called their attention.

I should like to record here my thanks to the successive Pepysian Librarians, Mr. V. S. Vernon Jones, Mr. Percy Lubbock, Mr. Stephen Gaselee, and Mr. O. F. Morshead, who have facilitated my work in every way possible to them.

M. R. JAMES.

Eton, *November*, 1922.

BRIEF LIST OF MANUSCRIPTS

	Date	Pepys's No.	Page
New Testament in English	xv	**15, 16**	1
Metrical Analysis of the New Testament	1596	**21**	2
Medica	xv	**878**	3
Receipts, etc.	xv	**1047**	5
Choir Office for a Bishop	xv	**1198**	6
Roger Bacon	xv	**1207**	7
Musica, etc.	xv	**1236**	8
On the Philosopher's Stone	xvii	**1295**	11
Medica	xv	**1307**	11
Libel of English Policy	xv	**1461**	12
Magica	xvi	**1530**	13
Horologion Slavonice	xvi	**1554**	14
Horae	xv	**1576**	14
Religious Poems in English	xv	**1584**	19
Guillaume de Machaut	xv	**1594**	24
Octateuch in English	xv	**1603**	26
Jean Mallart	xvi	**1607**	27
Medica	xiv	**1661**	29
Kalendar	xv	**1662**	31
Musica	xv–xvi	**1760**	36
Coronation Pageant of Queen Claude	1517	**1791**	38
Apocalypse in Latin and French	xiv	**1803**	40
Mediaeval Sketch Book	xiv–xv	**1916**	47
Vegetius, etc., in French	xiv	**1938²**	51
Sir John Mandeville	xv	**1955**	56
Tracts in Italian	xviii	**1998**	57
G. Wither	xvii	**1999**	58
Medulla Grammatices	xv	**2002¹**	59
Chaucerian Pieces	xv	**2006**	60
Scotch Survey of the Prayer-Book	xvii	**2007**	63
Lydgate: Book of Thebes	xv	**2011**	64

MEDIAEVAL MANUSCRIPTS

NEW TESTAMENT IN ENGLISH.
    C.M.A. 6750. 31.   **[15, 16.]**

Vellum, $5\frac{5}{8} \times 3\frac{1}{4}$, ff. 194 and 215, double columns of 26 lines. Cent.
xv (1437). Very well written, in a clear slightly sloping hand : black ink.

The binding is very beautiful, with imitation black and white inlay and
gold tooling on red. The fore-edges are ornamented with a pattern of
tulips and other flowers in colour on gold.

    I. $1^8 - 4^8$ 5^{10} $6^8 - 24^8$.
    II. $1^8 - 24^8$ (wants 4) $25^8 - 27^8$ (apparently).

Contents. The New Testament in English.
Vol. I. Here begynnyþ Mathew þe euangel of Ihesu Crist : þe firste
book of þe newe testement · þe first capit°.

At the end of John :
Here endiþ Jon þe euangel of Ihesu Crist þe laste of þe foure euangels.
Kalendar in Latin in red and black : Sarum.   170

Mar.	1, 2	Dauid, Cedde.
Ap.	29	Transl. S. Edmundi reg. et m.
May	4	Ioh. beuerlei.
	14	Teboldi.
June	9	Transl. S. Edmundi archiep. et C. ix lect. In red.
Oct.	4	Francii.
	12	Albri.
Nov.	2	Eustachio sociorumque eius. In red.
	17	Hugonis ep. C.

Ciclus concurrencium.   176
Here schewiþ a rewle of dyuerce þingis þat han be bifallen in
engelonde.   177

    þe · deer ʒeer · 1315 · þe greete deeþ · 1350 · þe romoure · 1381 ·
    þe erþe grone · 1382 · þe romoure of lordis · 1387 · *þe lepe ʒeer.*

Note þou þᵗ whanne þe ʒeeris of our lord mowen be departid euene, etc.
be rewle of þe chirche, etc.
To knowe of ester day þe rewle.
Similar rules ending with *Alleluia closiþ.*
This is þe rule of bookis, etc. List of the books of both Testaments.
Here biginneþ a rule þat telliþ in what chapeteris, etc.   179

B

Table of Gospels and Epistles de tempore and de Sanctis.

Thus endiþ þis kalender of lessonys pistlis & gospellis of al þe ȝere after þe vesse of salisberye.

On 194ᵇ: Whanne þe ȝeeris were of þe makinge of þe worlde · 6681 · and whanne þe ȝeers of our ⟨lord⟩ ihesu crist were of his incarnacioun · 1437 · þo was þis book writen.

The number 1437 is in black, and apparently written over another date in red which seems to end with a 6 : ? 1396 : 1437 would leave 5244 for the year B.C.: 1396 leaves 5295.

Vol. II. contains: Pauline Epistles.   I

Without Laodiceans.

Acts, 110. Cath. Epp. 166ᵇ. Apoc. 189.

A leaf is gone containing part of 2, 3 John and Jude.

There are no prologues.

Such ornament as occurs in the first volume and at the beginnings of the principal divisions of the second is of high quality: the rest poor. It is confined to initials and partial borders in gold and colour.

At least two scribes have been employed.

This copy is no. 124 in Forshall and Madden's list, and is there stated to be of the later version.

METRICAL ANALYSIS OF THE NEW TESTAMENT.
C.M.A. 6755. 36.   [21.]

Vellum, 4¾ × 3⅖, ff. 59, 32 lines to a page. Cent. xvi (1596), very neatly written.

With Pepys' usual binding: lettered Cont(ents) of N. Test.

On f. 1 are some Latin lines giving the order of the Biblical books.

1. The contents of the New Testament in metre:

The argument of the foure Evangelists   2
            In this History following,
            Of CHRIST his gospell pure :
            By Matthew, Marke, Luke and John,
            Sound witnesses and sure :

                    ·   ·   ·

            And nere the Citie Ephesus,
            In zeale and loving care,
            The same apostle buried was,
            As writers do declare.

The order of the Alphabet.   4

The plan of the book is to describe in a single stanza of 8 lines the contents of each chapter of each book of the N. T.: and the stanzas begin with A, B, C, etc., successively (a fresh alphabet beginning with each book) down to V. The alphabet then recommences if necessary, and the 21st chapter of a book will be denoted by AA.

Thus the stanza for Matt. i begins : A pedegre of Christ oure King : that for Matt. xxi thus : An Asse doth now our Saviour beare.

Arguments are prefixed to some of the books.

Apocalypse ends f. 47 :

> He tooke this payne, that thow might'st gayne,
> Let GOD haue all the praise. Amen.

This Booke was fynished the sixt Day of Aprile, in the yeare of oure Lord God 1596

> Per R. T. A° aetatis suae 63.
> Soli deo honor et gloria. Amen.

f. 47^b blank.

2. A collection of riddles in verse by the same author.   48

Preface :   Let not these toyes thyne eye offend,
Good Reader, I the pray :
That scribled are vpon viod (= void) leaves
Which next ensue though they :
Be placed here so nigh the book, etc.

There are 52 riddles ending on f. 56.

57, 58^a are blank.

3. Sibillarum oracula, viz. :   59

1. Sibilla Persica. Gignetur deus in orbem terrarum et gremium Virginis erit salus gentium, et pedes eius in valitudine hominum.
2. S. Libica. Ecce veniet dies et illuminabit dominus, etc.
3. S. Delphica. Nascetur propheta.
4. S. Cumana. Magnus ab integro.
5. S. Erythrea. In ultima aetate humiliabibur deus.
6. S. Samia. Ecce veniet diues.
7. S. Hellespontia. De excelso coelorum habitaculo.
8. S. Tyburtina. Nascetur Christus in Bethlehem—cuius ubera illum lactabunt.

MEDICA.

     C.M.A. 6802. 83.   **[878.]**

Vellum, $6\frac{5}{8} \times 4\frac{7}{8}$, ff. 96, 27 lines to a page. Cent. xv early : partly in a very excellent hand.

Collation : $1^8 \; 2^{10} \; (+1) \; 3^8 \; 4^{10} \; 5^8 \; 6^8 \; 7^{10} \; 8^8 - 11^8 \; (+1)$.

There are notes by Waterland on the fly-leaf, and a list of the contents.

1. Her begynnyth þe wyse boke of philosophye and aster (or after, *l.* astronomie) conteyned (*l.* contrevyd) and made of þe wysest philosophur and astronemo þᵗ euer was seth þᵉ world was first be gon þᵗ is to say of þᵉ lond of Grece ffor in þat lond an Englysch man fful wis was and wel

understandyng of philosophie & astronome stodied & compyled þᵉ boke out of grewe in to Englysche graciously.

Fyrst þis boke tellyth how many heuenys þer ben.

Ends unfinished p. 37 : he schal not drede þe palsye noþer þe rynnyng goote.

P. 38 blank.

Other copies in MS. Ashmole 189, 1443, and elsewhere.

2. Of Urines: in another hand.   39
Uryns brown wᵗ a blacke rynge, etc.
Change of hand on p. 42.

3. Various receipts: ffor þe morfu.   54
Change of hand at p. 59.

4. De Urinis.   Omnis urina est colamentum sanguinis.   108
              —dolorem in capite signat.

Corpus hominis ex quatuor humoribus constat   110
       —pacientes pleni uidentur.

List of remedies, alphabetical, in triple columns with notes of quantities.
      Ambra.   [113
      Acacia.
      Agarica.
Followed by Oils and Electuaries, and receipts.
English is resumed on p. 121.
Aqua vite perfectissima.   125
Natures of the xii signs : lucky and unlucky days.   126
Classification of materia medica according to the four qualities.   127
De calidis in primo gradu, etc.
A short dictionary of materia medica.   133
Aloen succus est herbe calidus, etc.
Ends with zucarum.
The first hand resumes on p. 152.
Receipts : ffor the mygryme, etc.   152
Directions for the seasons and months.   170
Followed by other receipts.   Virtues of " beteyne," etc.
Tract on the Plague (John of Bordeaux) without title.   187
The .1. capit. tellus how man schal kepe hym in tyme þerof.

Ending p. 192 : for to make poundir · and drede þe neuere þe pestelence.   Expl. liber.

Two later notes follow ; the second is mutilated.

RECEIPTS, ETC.
> C.M.A. 6801. 82. [1047.]

Paper, 7⅛ × 5¼, ff. 23, 19-20 lines to a page. Cent. xv late: well written. In wrapper of patterned paper. A single quire of 24 leaves, the 14th being cut out.

Contents

Rules for conduct (16 lines):

> Aryse erly & serue god devoutly 1
> And the worlde besyly
>
> . . . .
>
> And then slepe suverly
> This ffesyk is holi. Cf. *Book of St. Albans.* (s. 5)

Receipts: *a.* A medesyn for the stomake. *b.* ffor the toth ake. 1ᵇ
List of terms expressive of collections of animals or people. 2

> A herde of hertis . A herde of alle dere.

With one or two additions and corrections: ending 5ᵇ.

> A rawsclle of knaves · An vncredibilite of Cukkoldys.
> A dysworschip of scottis.
> Explicit Julyan Barne.

It contains 145 entries (including additions) as against 164 in "the Compaynys of beestys & fowlys" in the Book of St. Albans.

Various receipts, ffor the fflyx, ffor the steche, etc. 6
Gentyll manly Cokere and copyd of the Sergent to the kyng. 7

These culinary receipts continue to 13ᵇ. A slip is cut off the bottom of that leaf. On 13ᵇ is A charme for the blody flyx.

In nomine, etc. Stabat Ihesus contra flumen Iordanis, etc.

On 14 the culinary matter is continued: on 15ᵇ, 16 the receipts are in verse.

On 17-20 they are medical and miscellaneous.

On 21 are some relating to hawks.

On 22 : To chese an hauke gode.

Now ye moste lern the termys of haukyng. 22

Youre flyghte to þᵉ fenne ys when the hauke has founde hir game hir selfe, etc.

Eueryman after his degre. 22

> An Egylle ys moste worthyest for an Emperoure, etc.
>
> . . . .
>
> A musket for a holy water clerke.

A similar list in the Book of St. Albans.

There ben iiij bestys of venere, etc. (Also in the Book of St. Albans.)

Thes (i.e. the above) ben of the swete foote, etc. [22ᵇ

The fulmard, the fychew, etc.
—and all thes byn gamys of the stynkyng ffoote.
Here endys haukyng w^t medsyns and castyng
And all that longys to goode hauke kepyng.
Prognostics for the year according to the day of the week on which
Christmas falls.   23

> The yere that Cristysmas day fallyth on Sonday
> Yemps schall be gode vere wyndy Estas dry, etc.

Here ben the medys of the masse.   23^b
To hym that herys his masse & seys the blyssed lord in forme of
brede.
Ends imperfectly: and as long as thow arte.

CHOIR OFFICE FOR A BISHOP.
          C.M.A. vac.   [1198.]

Vellum, 7$\frac{1}{10}$ × 5, ff. 2 + 126 + 4, 24 lines to a page.   Cent. xv, in two
hands, the first of which is very good.   Written in England.

Plain calf binding, with Pepys' device : back gilt and lettered Offic.
Episc. in choro.

Collation : a^2 a^8–13^8 (wants 7, 8) 14^8–16^8 b^4.
On ii^b a list of contents (xv).

Contents :
Hic inc. seruicium de omni officio episcopali consernente chorum.
Primo quando episcopus incipit se parare ad celebrandum incipiatur
ab aliquo sacerdote de superiori gradu ista antiphona secundum usum
ecclesie anglicane cum psalmis subsequentibus.
Veni domine · Amen.   Notes on 4-line stave.
Quam dilecta · Benedicite · Inclina domine.   Credidi.   De profundis.
Ant. Veni domine uisitare, etc.
Celebracio ordinum die sabbati iiii^{or} temporum.
Litany, 4^b.   *Conf.* Swithin, Birinus.   *Virgins*, etc., end with Prisca, Tecla,
Affra, Editha, Anna.
Dedicacio ecclesie.   8^b
Hand changes at quire 3 (f. 17).
Deinde sequitur altarium consecracio.   22^b
In consecracione altaris sine ecclesia.   36^b
Benedictio lapidis portatilis.   38
Ordo qualiter reliquie ponende sunt in altare.   39^b
In consecracione cimiterii.   43^b
In reconciliacione ecclesie.   46

In consecracione episcopi.   57
In die cene.   52
Consecracio uirginis.   55
Hic inc. seruicium chori ad recludendum reclusum.   61
Ad campanam benedicendam.   68ᵇ
At f. 73, quire 10, the first hand resumes.
Ordo diei cinerum.   73
Dominica in ramis palmarum.   80
Feria v. in cena domini.   89
Feria vi. in parasceue.   93
Sabbato in vigilia pasche.   100ᵇ
In die pasche.   101ᵇ
At f. 103, quire 14, the second hand resumes.
In coronacione regis.   103
In consecracione s. crucis.   108
Ordo sepeliendi.   109ᵇ

This ends f. 126ᵇ. After the antiphon *Ego sum resurrectio* :

Require ps. supra in dedicacione ecclesie · deinde sequatur a choro Kyriel. (ter). *Postea prosequatur episcopus officium suum usque in finem et sic finitur seruicium sepulture.*

Constant reference is made to the Pontifical.
There is some nice ornament in the English style on ff. 1 and 73.

R. BACONIS QUAEDAM.
C.M.A. 6777. 58.   [1207.]

Vellum, 7⅕ × 5, ff. 77, 34 lines to a page. Cent. xv, in a very ugly and much contracted script.

Stamped binding: a roll consisting of square panels of ornament alternating with profile heads in medallions facing *l.*, one bareheaded, the second helmeted, the third in a sort of Phrygian cap.

2 f. ab eodem puncto (?).

Collation: 1¹² (+ 1*) 2 (one) 3¹⁶ 4¹² 5¹² 6⁸ (8 canc.) 7¹⁶.

1. At top of f. 1. Perspectiua Bachonis, etc. Ioannes Dee 1544 Oxoniae Tractatus perspectiue habens 3ᵉˢ partes prima est de communibus ad ceteras 2ᵃˢ 2ᵃ pars descendit in speciali ad visionem rectam, etc.

The diagrams are neatly drawn; some (about f. 55) occupy the whole page.

Ends 61ᵃ : rem visam p̄n̄t (possunt ?), etc., sicud (?) superius habetur.
Expl. perspectiua ffratris Rogeri Bakun.
Three short notes follow.

2. Title by Dee : Rogerius Bachon de multiplicatione specierum. 61ᵇ
Species multiplicata in me*di*o aliunde vocatur similitudo agentis—ideo
magis est actiua propter hoc quod est propinquior agenti.
Expl. tract. Bacon de multipl. specierum.

3. Physica Baconis.   74
Ut plenius intelligantur ymagines de ‚operibus seu orbibus septem
planetarum.
—et descripsi circa finem (?) litere (?) in qua manifestantur ea que dicta
sunt.
Expl. phisica Bacon satis subtiliter Deo gratias. (*quod griffith* added.)
Notes in a sixteenth-century hand, Super 1º ethicorum.   75ᵇ
On 77ᵇ are : *a.* A much obliterated note.
  b. Cantelena indictata per S. Stephanum Archiep. Cant. (xv.)
Cum sit omnis caro fenum   et post fenum fiat cenum   homo
quid extolleris.
Ends : Memento te moriturum   et post mortem id messurum
  quod hic seminaueris.
  c. Griffith de bangor.
  d. WS (monogram). Bangor.
  e. Diagram by Dr. Dee (?).
  f. Note (xvi–xvii). In this booke is seaventy & seaven written Leaves
begynnyng wᵗʰ Bacons perspectiue the wᵒʰ Mr. Jnº Collins is to Restore
me againe in like safe condition per me J. C (?). B . . . tes.
On the two fly-leaves at the end are sixteenth-century notes on
perspective.
The MS. is no. 41 in the list of Dee's MSS. (*Diary of Dr. Dee*,
Camden Soc., ed. Halliwell), p. 71.
" Rogerii Bachonis perspectiua.   Eiusdem de multiplicatione specierum
pergameno 4º.
In paste-boards with strings."
The strings are gone but the holes for them remain.
See A. G. Little, List of Roger Bacon's Works (App. to *Roger Bacon
Essays*, 1914), pp. 383, 387, and James, *Lists of Dee's MSS.*, Bibliogr. Soc.

MUSICA, ETC.
          C.M.A. vac.   [1236.]
Vellum paper, 7¼ × 5, various numbers of lines to a page. Cent. xv
? *cir.* 1460. Well written.
Collation : 1⁶ (+ 3) or 1¹⁰ (two canc. in 1st half) + 1 2¹² (11, 12 canc.)
3¹¹–5⁸ 6¹² 7¹⁰ 8⁸ 9⁸ 10¹²–13¹² (+ 1). Normally the outer and middle sheets
of each quire are of vellum. The modern foliation omits 2 ff.

The greater part of the contents is musical; and is described by Mr. Barclay Squire. The portions which have not to do with music are as follows:

ff. 7ᵇ 8ᵃ. Magna charta de libertatibus mundi, dated 2 Feb. 1637.
Christ hath cancelled the writeinge of all mans deth, etc.
A later form of a mediaeval fancy called Charta salutis, or the like.
8ᵇ 9ᵃ blank. On 9ᵃ. Thomas Keen (xvii).
10. A Paschal Table for the years 1460 to 1519.
87ᵇ. Rules for diet for the year.
Thys techith Galyen the good leche to alle maner of men & wymmen. How they shalle vse here metis and drynkys yn alle the monethes in the yere.
Prognostics for the year according to the Sunday letter.   88ᵇ
A. An hoot wynter. A somer wᵗ tempestes, etc.
Here folowᵗ the vertues of the Edder skyn.   89
Various receipts for tricks.   89ᵇ
Predictions:

> When feythe fayleth in prestys sawys
> & lordys wylle be londys lawys, etc.
>
> When gonewey shalle on curtays calle
> Then Wallys shall rayke and hastely ryse
> Then Albeon skottlonde shall to hem falle
> then waken wonders in euery wyse, etc.

Carleton Brown, *Register of Middle English Religious . . . Verse,* no. 2525.
The condycyons that be in man.
    The lyuer maketh a man to loue.
    The longys cawsyth the tonge to speke, etc.
On 93–95ᵃ are tables of planets and *Etas lune* and directions for making some sort of dial, with a diagram.   94ᵇ
At 95 a distich on the emblems of the Evangelists.
And some notes in English (xvi–xvii) for finding Easter.
Hymn to the Virgin with refrain *Maria virgo virginum*: 12-line stanzas.
                                                            [98ᵇ

> Regina celi and lady letare
> Lemyng lely and in place of lyght
> Quia quem meruisti portare
> Ye ben sett sempiterne in his syght, etc.

Ending:

> O quene fulle quene to euery creature
> pray that we may to the com
> to se thy trone and thy tresoure
> Maria virgo virginum.

Carleton Brown, l.c., no. 1723 (only this MS. cited).

A short tract on music.   104

De Epitrito et Epogdon.   Epitritus est figura et pertinet et accentum.

With musical illustrations.

Ends with a series of musical illustrations to which this rubric is prefixed.

Ostendam vobis punctu[r]arum diuersarum proportionem diuersis modis propter erudientiam.   107b

Another tract on music.   109

Musica docet de numero sonoro primi autem inspectores huius artis primo perceperunt conuenienciam soni per percussionem malleorum.

Ends with a diagram of Numerus multiplicatus malleorum.   110

Stans puer ad mensam.   110b

Latin distich or quatrain and English version.

> In maner whyche enlumineth euery astate
> to discerne the doctrine chylde geue attendaunce.

Ends:

> among them þᵗ ben of þᵉ contre of fame
> he taught me this grostede was is name.

This does not appear to be among the versions printed in Furnivall's *Babees Book*, E.E.T.S.   Carleton Brown, no. 909 (only MS. cited).

The Age of the Moon.   Carleton Brown, no. 2136.   114b

> The furst day of þᵉ mone
> God wyst well what was to done } Adam þᵗ day he made
>
> .   .   .   .
>
> and loke þⁿ be ware of euery day }
> and þⁿ shalt spede welle in fay   } this sayde an astronomer.

English notes (xvi) on the same page (120b).

On 127b three 7-line stanzas: speeches of Jeremias, Ysayas, Dauid. "A liturgical text of the prophecies of the advent, in rime royal."

> O ye pepill of ierusalem be holde and se
> make your respect into the orient
> a kyng is comyng of gret poste, etc.

Carleton Brown, l.c., no. 1602 (only this MS. cited).

The last four lines of the third stanza are washed out, and a late quatrain (xvii) written in:

> On a crucifix
> Why not the picture of our dying Lord
> as of a friend nor this nor that adored
> does not the Eternal law command that thou
> shalt euen as well forbeare to make as bow.

On 128ª (xv) :

> In · 8 · is all my loue ⎫
> and · 9 · be sette by fore ⎪
> so · 8 · be yclosyd aboue ⎬ Iħc
> than · 3 · is good there fore ⎭

ON THE PHILOSOPHER'S STONE.

C.M.A. 6785. 66. [1295.]

Paper, 7½ × 6⅕, pp. 68, 29 lines to a page. Cent. xvii. Fairly written ; paper discoloured.

Slip covers, with marbled paper.

A Discourse of the Philosopher's stone.

The matter of the Philosopher's stone together with the Manner of workinge to be obserued in the preparation of the same ys simplie one, etc.

Ends p. 63 : Archanum Maximum et donum dei altissimi to whome for all his Mercies & Bounties be ascribed euerlastinge praise and thanckes. Amen.

Heere endeth this treatise composed in Germania anno Restauratae Salutis 1613.

Some additions in the same hand occupy pp. 63-8, including an *Aenigma Philo(so)phicum* in verse.

> Created was I with the ffriste
> Am found in euerythinge
> In high in lowe in heauen & earthe
> and in all thinges moouinge, etc.

MEDICA.

C.M.A. vac. [1307.]

Vellum, 7½ × 5⅛, 25 lines to a page, ff. 64 + 1. Cent. xv, well written with plain red initials.

Collation : 1⁸ 2⁶ 3⁸-8⁸ (+ 2 after 2nd), 1 fly-leaf.

1. A list of remedies and receipts in alphabetical order.

Aurea alexandrina ℞ Azarabacca Carpobalsami henbelle seed englysche ganyngale.

Ends with zinzeberum conditum.

& boyle it & do it in a gene potte and wryte hys name.

From Nicholaus Anglicus?

2. Here begynnyn þe vertuys of þis antitorie Nicho*lai* & Mesue.   41

Aure Alexandrina is good for þe wynde in þe hed.

Ends with Zynzebere conditum.

—wᵗ dia saturion and dia margaton and oþer.

3. Here begynnith þe namis of alle þe erbis þᵗ longᵗ to helthe of man.
Arthemesia mater herbarum mogwort.   [51
Absinthium wermod.
Ends unfinished in P.
57ᵇ, 58ᵃ blank. Some notes on 58ᵇ.

4. Here þow schalt knowe alle maner of urinys.   59
This tract continues to the end.

LIBEL OF ENGLISH POLICY.
C.M.A. 6817. 98.   [1461.]

Vellum, $7\frac{7}{8} \times 5\frac{3}{4}$, ff. 30, 29 lines to a page. Cent. xv late.
In paste boards covered with green and gold paper.

Collation: 1^8–3^8 4^6.

1. Here begynnyth the prologe of the processe of the libell of englysch policie exhortyng all England to kepe the see enviroun and namly the narow see seyng what profyt cometh ther of and all so what worschype and saluacocioun (!) to Engeland.   1

> The trewe processe of Englisch policie
> Vttward to kepe this reame in rest.

(A ballad in seven 7-line stanzas, ending)
> ther for y bygyn to wrete now of the see.

The poem begins:
> Of the Commodytes of Spayn & flawnders   2
> Commodites i callyd comynge owt of spayne
> Know well all men that profyte yn certeyne, etc.

Of the Commodites of Pruce, high duchemen and Esterlyng*es*.   6
Of the Commodytes of Braban, Seland, Henaute, etc.   11
'Irlond' and Wales, f. 13.
Conclusyon of kepynge of the narow see by a storye of kynge Edgar & ij Incydent*is* of kynge E. the iii*th* & kynge Henr. the v.   17
Of Unyte.   21
End: When he the radde all*e* ouyr manyght
> Go forthe trew boke & Cryst defend the ryght.

Expl. libellus de policia conceruatiua maris.
23ᵇ blank.
Last printed in *Political Poems*, Wright, Rolls Series, ii. 157 from other MSS. It belongs to the class of copies in which Lord Hungerford's name occurs in the last stanza. See further a correspondence in *Times Lit. Supp.* 1922.

2. In a larger and worse hand.
Receipts and directions for assaying. 24
To Syment golde. 25^b

3. The Endenture of Kyng Edwarde the thyrde. 26^b
With regard to standard of gold.
Followed by further matter about assaying.

On the two last leaves are a few ill-written entries, apparently accounts. John Whytte of y⁰ berstrete is mentioned and a few other names occur.

MAGICA.

C.M.A. 6799. 80. [1530.]

Paper, 8⅜ × 6⅛, ff. 25, 28 lines to a page. Cent. xvi, clearly written. In a cover of patterned paper.

A collection of Magical Formulae: mostly in English.

1. To spirits guarding a hidden treasure.
2. "This fyrste." A prayer for the same, or for summoning the spirit into a crystal.
3. To the Holy Ghost: for the same.
4. Shorter prayers, and a conjuration of the spirit, to appear in the crystal.
5. Latin form: the spirit to depart from a house.
6. Coniuratio malignorum spirituum in corporibus hominum existentium. Gospels in Latin and Latin prayers, partly glossed in English.
7. Love philtres. Here and elsewhere the vowels are expressed by numbers, e.g. pr4 1m4r2 = pro amore.
f. 17 blank.
8. Conjuration. The spirit to appear in the crystal in the shape of a man childe of ten years.
9. The byndynge of the spirite.
10. Further receipts. Pro amore, to fynde to be invicible, ad furem inveniendum, with diagram of circle.
Pro libro et claue.
To knowe the truthe. Three circles, two with Hebrew letters, the other divided into degrees; engraved, pasted on.
Pro spatula.
11. The planets.
12. Three diagrams of magical circles, with the places of the officiants marked.
13. A conjuration in English.

HOROLOGION SLAVONICE.
C.M.A. vac.
[1554.]

Paper, $7\frac{3}{5} \times 5\frac{7}{10}$, ff. 159, 13 lines to a page.   Cent. xvi.

Binding, stamped red leather over wooden boards: among the stamps are a dragon in a lozenge and a griffin in a square.   Two clasps.

Collation: 1^8 (wants 1, 2) 2^8–18^8 (6 canc.) 19^8 20^{12} (11, 12 canc.).

In seven divisions, each of which has a panel of ornament at the beginning in red, green, purple, white, rather roughly executed.

i. f. 1.   ii. f. 16.   iii. f. 61.   iv. f. 92.   v. f. 119.   vi. f. 139.   vii. f. 147^b.

It is a *Horologion*, of the Greek rite, in Slavonic.

There is no date or name attached.

A printed edition of the same, of 1597, is in the library of King's College.

HORAE.
C.M.A. 6758. 39.
[1576.]

Vellum, $7\frac{7}{8} \times 5\frac{3}{4}$, ff. 170, 18 lines to a page.   Cent. xv (*cir.* 1480); in a good upright hand.   In Pepys' binding.

Collation: 1^{12} 2^8–6^8 (wants 3) 7^8 8^8 9^6 10^8–21^8 (+1).

Contents.   Kalendar in red, blue, and gold.   1

Sequences of the Gospels.   13

Obsecro te, 17^b.   O intemerata, 20^b.

Septem gaudia.   Virgo templum trinitatis.   22^b

Septem gaudia spiritualia que modo habet in paradiso composita a b. thoma martire cantuariensi.   Gaude flore virginali.   25^b

Aue cuius conceptio, 27.   Alma redemptoris mater, 28.

On 25^b the name ' S. Margareta regina' written in the margin.

On 29^b a prayer added.   Beatissime d. I. C. respice super me miserum.

Hours of the Virgin (Use of Sarum).   29

Memoriae: the Holy Ghost, the Trinity, the Cross, St. Michael, John Baptist, Peter and Paul, Andrew.

On 46^b additions: *a* Aue maria ancilla trinitatis

                Auete omnes anime

                Sanc geor

        b Sancta Elizabeht

                Sanctus monanus.

Memoriae of St. George 47, Stephen, Laurence, Sebastian, Nicholas, Anthony, Anne, Magdalene, Katherine, Margaret, All Saints.

Matins of the Cross.   52

Additions: In nomine d. I. C. facio hoc signum tau crux rex venit in pace.   53

Prime of the Virgin, 53ᵇ, etc., to Compline.

After Salve regina: quinque gaudia de b. Marie.　Gaude uirgo mater Christi.　　72

Oratio de b. Maria composita a b. Bernardo.　Memento obsecro dulcis mater.　72ᵇ

Addition: Memoriae of several saints, viz. Denis, Christopher, George, Blasius, Giles, Martha (? M'te), Katherine, Margaret, Barbara, Ursula. 73ᵇ

Seven Psalms, Psalm of Degrees, and Litany.　　74

Additions: Prayer to St. Anne, attached to the Ave Maria.　Note of indulgence conceded for it by Alexander VI (10,000 years for mortal, 20,000 for venial sins).　　74ᵇ

Prayer.　Aue sanctissima maria mater dei . . . tu concepta sine peccato. Indulgenced by Sixtus (20,000 years).　　75

Testamentum Iulii pape secundi ad pulsum pa*cis* (? or pat*ris*) Octoginta milia annorum de quo habentur firme papalium literarum bulle.

O gloriosissima regina misericordie.　　75ᵇ

Collect for S. Duthac: D. d. omnip. qui semper clamantes ad te quamuis indigni sint tamen exaudis exaudi nos famulos tuos aures tue benignitatis pulsantes ut intercessione b. Duthaci confessoris tui atque pontificis apud te perpetuam mereamur habere mansionem.　　76ᵇ

Collect for S. Monan: Deus qui b. monanum confessorem tuum . . . infirmitatibus sanitatem restituis, etc.

Vigilie mortuorum.　　92ᵇ

Addition: Memoria: Kentigernus sub seruano gloriose studuit, etc.

At top of page: S. Cuthbertus.　S. Lucia.　　[115ᵇ

Commendatio animarum.　　116

Hoc scriptum fuit repertum rome retro altare b. petri, etc. (Indulgence of John XII).　Auete omnes anime.　　129

On 130 scribbled: S. Romanus.　S. Maria egipciaca.

On 130ᵇ: O martine o pie, etc.

The Fifteen Oo's.　　131

Psalmi de passione.　　139ᵇ

Prayer: O bone Ihesu.　　144ᵇ

Beatus gregorius dum esset summus pontifex . . . apparuit ei dominus Ihesus sub passionis effigie, etc.　O d. I. C. adoro te.　　146

D. I. C. qui septem verba.　　148

Or. ad d. I. C. in cruce pendentem.　Gloriosa passio.　　149ᵇ

Addition: Memoria of St. Apollonia against toothache.　　149ᵇ

Omnibus consideratis.　Prayers to the Five Wounds, the Cross, the Virgin, St. John.　　150

Addition: D. I. C. pater dilectissime.　　155ᵇ

Psalterium b. Iheronimi.　　156

Additions: De S. Marnano.   Deus qui es vita in te credentium.   157
         De S. C(i)arano.   Deus omnium creator et rector.
         De S. Palladio. 157^b
         De S. Seruano.   158
         De S. Beano. 158^b
         De S. Regulo.   159
         De S. Drostano. 159^b
         De S. Andrea.   160
         Deus qui preclara salutifere crucis.   168
         Repleto alimonio celesti.

In a better hand: Aue primas Anglorum O Edmunde confessorum (Memoria of St. Edmund of Canterbury).

In a hand not appearing elsewhere: Lydgate's " Compleynt that Crist maketh of his Passioun," in Scottish dialect. 170^b

The first two stanzas of this occur in Brit. Mus. Add. 31042 f. 94^b, and were printed by Heuser in the *Bonner Beiträge zur Anglistik*, xiv. 210. Note by Professor Carleton F. Brown, who adds that the version in our MS. is distinctly older and in an extreme northern dialect. See his *Register of Middle English Religious Verse*, no. 1301.)

O luue tyll restor þi expellence and loss
Frome paradyce place off most plessance
þe to raforme I hange apoñe þe corss
Cronit wy^t thorñe and wondit (with) a lanss
Handis & feit incressyñe my greuanss
Wy^t scharp nalis my blude maide ryning doune
Luk oñe my wondis & thynk oñe my passioñe

Thynk & remembyr oñe my bludy face
þe red stronge asell megit wy^t the gall
þe fell rabutynge mañe for þi traspass
þe huge full spettynge apoñe my wesage fall
Kynge of iewis in schorñe þe cañe me call
Bundynge & beffat be falss derissioñe
Mañe in þi comfort amange þi trubyllis all
Thynk on þe wall þat want in sondyr þañe

Oñe caluari quheñ I gaffe wp þe gost
In lik figwre to þe pellicañe
Thrange to þe hart bledynge in euere cost
Pail & dedly quhyll all my blud wes lost
þus off my garment throngyñe wp and & [*sic*] doñe
Vn to mischeyffe quheñ þow art trowbillit most
Luk oñe wondis & thynk oñe my passioñe
þe byttyr skalus (? sh- ? str-) off my mortalle sufferance

Remembyr off þar wnfrendy kyndnes
þe rude rapis strenʒit wy^t gret peñance
My tendyr lymmys maid fant wy^t febilness
Bunde tyll a pellar be wiolent sturdiness

> To mak a syarte for þi transgressioñe
> ffor scheff comfort in warldis distress
> Luk oñe my wondis & thynk oñe my passioñe
> The cressed is borne wyᵗ mony lyᵗ lantrene
> Suerdis staffys & stanis importabill
> Cryande terandly hydwyss.

It is quite clear that the book was produced in France for use by a Scotchman or in Scotland. The Kalendar contains many Scottish saints.

The following entries are noteworthy:

Jan. 9. Felani C. 13. Kentegerni Ep. 30. Transl. S. Anne.
Feb. 15. Fastini M. 17. Germanici. 28. Osualdi Ep.
Mar. 1. Albini Amandi. 3. Mature (*sic*) Ep. C. 6. Baldredi Ep. 9. Constantini reg. m. 16. Huberti Ep. 17. Patricii Ep. 18. Eduuardi reg. m. *in gold*. 19. Ioseph iusti. 20. Cuthberti Ep. 24. Dongardi Ep. C. 28. Rogati m. 31. Albine V.
Apr. 3. Ricardi Ep. 13. Maronis et Victo(ris) m. 21. donanus abbas *added*.
May 2. Florencii C. 4. festum corone domini. 5. Gotardi Ep. C. 16. Honorati Ep. m. 19. Dunstani Ep. *in gold*. 21. inuerialis (Iuuenalis) Ep. 26. Augustini angl. apost. *in gold*.
June 3. Erasmi Ep. m. 10. Ursini Archiep. 13. Antonii c. padue urbis. 17. Ranerii C. 20. Transl. eduuardi reg. m. 22. Paulini Ep. C.
July 2. Visitacio B. m. *in gold* with octave. 3. Martialis Ep. C. 7. Transl. S. Thome Cant. *in gold*. 8. Kiliani m. 16. Generosi C. 26. Anne not in gold.
Aug. 5. Osuualdi reg. m. 12. Clare V. 25. Ludouici C. 30. Fiacri C. 31. Transl. Niniani Ep.
Sept. 4. Transl. S. Cuthberti. 10. Nicholai de tolentino. 12. Helie Abb. 16. Niniani Ep. 24. Geremari Abb. 25. Firmini Ep. C.
Oct. 4. Francisci C. 5. In margin. Obitus Iohannis domini hay de ȝestyr a° dⁿⁱ m°. vᶜ. viij°. 12. Vuilfridi Archiep. 22. Melloni Archiep. 23. Romani Archiep. 24. Martini Abb. Verton.
Nov. 16. Eadmundi Arch. *in gold*. 18. Mandeti Abb. 19. Helizabeth matrone. 21. Columbini Abb. 30. Passio S. Andree *in gold*, with octave.
Dec. 8. Conceptio b. m. *in gold*. 17. Lazari Ep. Marthe V. 18. Graciani Ep. C. 22. Theodosie V. 23. Victorie V. 30. Supplicii Ep.

At top of f. 13 (lined through): This Booke perteine to Johñe Laflyn of.

The additions seem to be divided between the writer of this and the writer of the Obit of John Lord Hay.

In the Litany : *Martyrs* : Thoma, Albane, Eadmunde, Eduuarde, Osuualde.
Confessors : Dunstane, Gildarde, Medarde, Albine, Amande, Cuthberte, Hugo, Niniane, Columbane, Swynthine, Francisce.
Virgins : Columbana, Editha, Etheldedra (!), Brigida, Elizabeth, Affra, Genouefa.

Decoration. This is of ordinary late French character with a large amount of fluid gold. Every page has a piece of border the height of the text, with spotted ground of partly conventional and partly natural foliage and flowers.

c

In the Kalendar each month is illustrated by two pictures: occupation in *r.* border, sign of Zodiac in lower margin:

1-24. *Jan.* At table, back to fire: a servant on *l.* with dish.
Aquarius in stream with two jugs.
Feb. Warms his feet at fire: a man enters on *r.* with faggots.
Pisces in stream.
Mar. Two men prune vines in enclosure.   Aries.
Apr. In wattled field: young man with flowers hands one to seated lady who is making a wreath.   Taurus.
May Youth rides to *l,* hawk in hand, on white horse: lady behind him on pillion.   Gemini (apparently with one leg apiece) embrace.
June Man mows, woman rakes.   Cancer, a crayfish.
July Man reaps, another binds sheaves.   Leo.
Aug. One threshes, another winnows.   Virgo with flower.
Sept. One treads grapes, another brings grapes in a *hotte.*   Libra, held by a maiden.
Oct. Man sows, woman bears a sack on her back.   Scorpius.
Nov. Man beats oaks for pigs: woman on *l.* with distaff.   Sagittarius, a centaur, shooting back to *r.*
Dec. Houses forming two sides of a square. A man kills a pig with the back of an axe. In front another kneels on a slaughtered pig, and a woman holds a dish at its throat. Bundles of straw in front. Capricorn, a white goat.

25-8. *Sequence of the Gospels.* Illustrated by four small pictures, in the text, of the Evangelists writing, with their emblems.

29. *Obsecro te.* Large. The Virgin and Child throned. Two angels in air crown her: two kneeling *r.* and *l.* play harp and pipe (?). Rubbed.

30. *O intemerata.* In text. Pietà, with two holy women kneeling *r.* and *l.*

31. *Virgo templum.* In text. The Virgin carried upward by four angels. Rubbed.

32. *Matins.* Large. Annunciation: the Virgin kneels on *l.* The dove on ray. Gabriel with scroll (*ave-tecum*).

33. *Lauds.* Large. Visitation: the Virgin on *l.* attended by two angels. Rubbed.

34. *Memoriae.* In text. Italian Trinity: starry sky behind.
35.   (The Cross). Christ bearing the Cross.
36.   Michael and the devil.
37.   John Baptist with lamb.
38.   Peter with keys, Paul with sword.
39.   Andrew with saltire cross.
40.   Large. George on white horse (facing *l.*) with raised sword, Dragon below, his neck pierced with broken lance. Princess kneels by city gate on *r.*
41.   In text. Stephen with stone on head and in hand.
42.   Laurence with gridiron.
43.   Two men shooting arrows at Sebastian.
44.   Nicholas: 3 children in tub.
45.   Anthony with staff, rosary, and pig.
46.   Anne teaching the Virgin to read.
47.   Magdalene with casket.
48.   Katherine with sword and wheel.
49.   Margaret emerging from dragon.
Small miniature for Matins of the Cross cut out.

50. *Prime*. Large. The Virgin and people adore the Child. Two angels in *c.* Shepherds in doorway on *r.* Ox and ass feed at rack on *l.*

51. *Tierce*. Two shepherds are kneeling. Woman plaits wreath. Angels have scroll with music (*Gloria-deo*).

52. *Sext*. Adoration of the kings. Joseph absent.

53. *Nones*. Presentation. Symeon nimbed (and another man) on *l.* Anna and the maid behind the Virgin.

54. *Vespers*. Flight, to *l.* Maid following. Soldier and husbandman in the background.

55. *Compline*. Coronation. The Virgin kneels on *l.* A small angel crowns her: two more behind. The Son throned on *r.* with orb.

56. *Seven Psalms*. David kneels by throne (*r.*), harp on altar (with white cloth) before him. God seen in the sky. Rubbed.

57. *Vigil of the dead*. Three youths on horseback on *l.* in consternation: three corpses on *r.* City wall on *l.*, and gold churchyard cross in background.

58. *Commendatio*. In front two men lay shrouded corpse in a grave. Coped and surpliced clergy, and black-cloaked and hooded women.

59. *Auete*. Last judgment. On *l.* the Virgin and John Ev., on *r.* John Baptist and Peter. Two angels with trumpets. Three dead rising.

60. *xv oo's*. The Crucifixion, with the thieves. The Virgin swoons on *l.* Jews and soldiers on *r.* Rubbed.

61. *Prayer*. *Od. I. C. adoro te*. Mass of St. Gregory. Christ on the altar supported by an angel. Instruments of the Passion form a background on *l.* Cock on column, hammer, pincers, purse, tunic, cross, reed, lance. Two servers kneel. In the *r.* corner the pieces of money and the dice. Rubbed.

62. *Omnibus consideratis*. Christ wounded carrying the cross, with title, and with His hand to His side. He stands in a tent of red curtains, green inside, held back by two angels.

63. *Psalter of Jerome*. Jerome in Cardinal's robes standing in room, with palm and book; his lion on *l.* fawns on him.

John Lord Hay of Yester appears first as a Lord of Parliament (for Scotland) in 1487. The title is now merged in that of Tweeddale. No. 1584 belonged to the same family.

RELIGIOUS POEMS IN ENGLISH.
C.M.A. 6787. 68.
[1584.]

Paper (and vellum), $8\frac{1}{10} \times 5\frac{1}{2}$, ff. 3 + 111, 25 lines to a page. Cent. xv. In rather current hand.

Collation: 3 vellum fly-leaves (2, 3 being a sheet); 1^{20} (1 canc.) 2^{20} 3^{16} 4^{20} 5^{20} (+1) 6^{16} (wants 16: 15 stuck to vellum fly-leaf).

The first fly-leaf is a part of a leaf of a service book (xiv), with fragment of the Office for Corpus Christi and Trinity.

ff. ii, iii (xv) have the following matter:

Obitus d^ni georgii de cunyngam de beltoñe A.d. M.CCC. (cut) lxxxii° (doubtless 1482) xxviii° mensis Iulii. Ob. thome hay fil. . . . et apparens Ihoannis hay de ʒestir qui obiit xxvii° die mensis . . . Iunii A. d. mill. cccc° lxxxxj°.

Obitus mag^ri andree hay prepositus quondam ecclesie de . . . nis qui obiit xvi° die mens. Ian. A. D. M° CCCC . . .

Obitus Wil^{mj} hay filius domini de ȝestyr qui ob. septimo die mens. Iul. A. d. M°cccc° nonagesimo . . .

Charm against fever.

In nomine, etc.   Ante portam ierusalem iacebat S. petrus.   Ecce Ihesus veniens petre quid hic iaces, etc.

On ii^b iii^a.   Nobis sancte spiritus gratia sit data
De qua virgo virginum fuit obumbrata, etc.

Veni sancte spiritus omnipotens sempiterne
Suum sanctum spiritum deus eligauit.
In die pentecostes suos confortauit.

On the lower margins and on iii^b (mostly covered by the book-plate) prayers are added, I think, in the same hand which has made the later set of additions in the *Horae*, no. 1576, which also belonged to the Hays of Yester.

On iii^b.   Liber Iohannis Lesly de eodem, etc.

f. 1. This litill boke is compilid of full notabill & prophetabill sentencis to stir and to edifie them y^t redith in it to gode conuersation and gydyng. And theis bene the matirs.

1. The compleynt of god.
2. The myrrour of mankynd.
3. The sele of mercy.
4. The lesouns of dirige y^t is clepid peti Joob.
5. The prouerbis of salomon.
6. The merkis of meditatiouns.
7. The prophetis of erthely angyr.
8. A salutatioun of our lady.
9. The x commaundementis.
10. The vij werkis of mercy bodili and gostly.
11. The v wittis bodili and gostly.
12. The vij dedly synnys.
13. The vij vertuous contrari to þo synnys.
14. The iiij doweris of the bodi
     And iiij of the soule.
     Torne the to this side of the lefe.
     And ther be gynnyth first the
     Compleynt of god and so folowyng
     euery matir oon aftir a nodir.

1. The compleynt of god, by William Lychefelde : see Furnivall, *Political, Religious, and Love Poems.* E.E.T.S. Ed. 1, p. 168, ed. 2, p. 190. Carleton Brown, *Register,* no. 1672.   [1^b

Oure gracyous god prince of pite
Whois myght and godenes neuer be gan
      .   .   .   .   .
That to þ^l chosyn ordenyd is
That leuyth syn and them amend.

Here endith the compleynt of god
And begynnyth the myrrour of mankynde.

2. The merour of mankynde. Furnivall, *Hymns*, etc. E.E.T.S., 1887 and 1895, p. 58. Carleton Brown, no. 779. [14

> Howe mankynde dothe be gyn
> Is wondir to discryve so
>
> . . .
>
> To Mary moder maydon fre
> As sche bare a childe comfort to vs
> On þat soule hauen pite
> If it be the will of swete Ihesus. Amen.

Here endith, etc.

3. The seale of mercy (variant of Th. Brampton's *Seven Penitential Psalms* : Carleton Brown, no. 232, 964) 28

> As I lay in my bed
> And sikenes revid me of my rest
> What maner life yᵗ I had led
> ffor to thynke me thoughte it best.

Burden, *Ne reminiscaris domine*, corrected throughout from *Parce mihi domine*.

> . . .
>
> Whan I wᵗ god to þe blis schall wend
> That joy and blis he vs send
> That sched his blode vppon þᵉ tre
> And all þᵗ makith your last end
> With *Parce* etc. *Ne reminiscaris domine*.

Her endith, etc.

4. Pety Ioob, printed from Douce MS. 322, by Dr. Kail; *Twenty-six Poems*. E.E.T.S., 1904, p. 120. Carleton Brown, no. 1155. [48

> *Parce michi domine.*
> A leue lord my soule þⁿ spare
> The sothe I sey nowe sikirle (sikule)
>
> . . .
>
> Nowe fro þat lond þᵗ namyd is hell
> Worschipfull lord rescue me
> So that I may euer wᵗ þe dwell
> Thoroughe *Parce michi domine.*

Her endith, etc.

5. The proverbis of Salamon. Carleton Brown, no. 2484. 62

> Waste bryngith a kyngdome in nede
> Nede makith a man travaile
> The moar travell þᵉ moar mede
> So he do by gode comceile
>
> . . .
>
> Wᵗ his frendis oft will he fight
> And wᵗ his Enmy he dare not do so
> And takith his frendis gode agayn right
> To fend hym þer wᵗ agaynst his fo.

Here endith, etc.

· 6. The markis of meditacion (Stimulus Conscientiae Minor.   Carleton
Brown, no. 156.   Horstmann, *York Writers*, ii. 36).   [78ᵇ

> Al myghty god in trinite
> ffadir & sonne & holy gost. . . .

l. 9.   He may be clepid wise & witty
>   That can wele leve in this exile

>   ·   ·   ·   ·   ·

> *Nihil est vita mortalis nisi mors viuens*, etc.
> All oure life þat we here lede
> Is no thyng but a dethe lyvyng.

(On f. 81 : Abiuro episcopum Romanum Et omnes eius actus peruersos.)
In 6 chapters : The rubric of the last begins : *In omnibus operibus tuis
inenitur* (?) *iusticia et misericordia*, and ends : *In die uero Iudicii iusticia
dei erit aperta et misericordia occulta.*

f. 92 has two stanzas only in a different script, and the verso is blank ;
but the headline is uniform with the rest.

The poem ends :
> The rightwisnes of god wer than
> Oanly schewid and mercy nought.

Here endith, etc.

7. The xij profettis that men may gette in suffryng of bodyly anger.
Carleton Brown, no. 167.   [97

> Almyghty god þᵗ made all thyng
> Aftir his own ordynaunce
> Make us buxom to his biddyng
> And of our giltis graunte vs Repentaunce

>   ·   ·   ·   ·   ·

> And for hym specially ye pray
> That this tretice in to englische drewe
> That he hym schilde þᵗ on gode friday
> The Jewis naylid on þe Rode and flewe (slewe)
> And grawnt us life þᵗ last schall ay
> In hevyn þer Joy is euer newe.   Amen.

8. Salutacyon of oure lady.   Carleton Brown, no 649.   102ᵇ
(A scribbled name at top.)   John St . . .

> Heile fairist þᵗ euer was founde
> heile modir and mayden fre
> Heile floure of Ioseph wounde
> Heile þᵉ frute of Jesse.

>   ·   ·   ·   ·

> That we in heuyn may haue a sete
> And duell wᵗ þᵉ blissid floure.   Amen.

9. The x commaundementis.   Cf. Furnivall's *Hymns*, etc. p. 106 (107).
Carleton Brown, no. 838.   [104^b]

I warne euery man þᵗ lyvith in lond
And do hym dredles oute of were

Who so will to hevyn go
Kepe þem all breke noan of þo.

10. The vij werkys of mercy that euery man & woman shalbe examined
of at þe day of dom.   Mᵗ. xxvᵗᵒ.   Carleton Brown, no. 910 (only this copy
cited).   [105

In matheus gospell as we fynde
Whan crist schall cum in maieste

And all þᵗ hauen had charite
And did releve to nedy men
Schall euer in blis a bide wᵗ me
And þer to we schull say Amen.

Thes byn the vij werkys of mercy goostely.   Bülbring in Herrig's *Archiv.*
86. 389.   Carleton Brown, no. 2085.   [106^b]

Teche euery man wᵗ charite
to kepe goddis hestis buxom to be

Of their workis gostly crist schall appele
Whan he his dome schall deme & dele.

11. Thes be the v wittis bodely.   Bülbring, l.c. 388.   Carleton Brown,
no. 1120.   [107

Kepe thy sight fro vanite
That þⁿ coveite not þᵗ evil may be

Theis ben þᵉ wittis fyve
That cristyn men schulde rule in lyve.

Þise be þe fywe wyttis gostly.   Carleton Brown, no. 692.   107^b

Haue mynde on þe blis þᵗ nevir schall blyn

That helpith a man to heuyn.

12. The vij dedly synnys.   Heuser, *Bonn. Beitr.* xiv. 205.   Carleton
Brown, no. 1705.   [107^b]

Pride is hed of all maner syn
That makith mannys soule from god to twyn.

Theis be þe synnys sevyn
That Reuyn men þe blis of hevyn.

13. Here sueth þe vij vertuous a gayn þe vij dedly synnys.   Carleton
Brown, no. 2666.   [108^b]

Aga(y)n pride.   With scharp thornys þ^t wer full kene

My hed was crownyd ye may well sene

.   .   .   .   .

That þeis lessouns will ouyr Rede

And þer w^t þair soulis fede.   Amen.

14. Here folowith þe iiij dowerys þe whiche þe bodies of all crist*is* true servaunt*is* schull be dowed in þe blis of hevyn aftir þe day of dome.   109

(In prose).   Here it wer for to speke of joy that men have in blis · and all if poule þ^t was Ravesschid saithe þ^t this joy is hid, etc.

The dowers of the soul, 110^b.   (I do not find it in Carleton Brown.)

f. 111^b is pasted over.   The last words are

of suche goodis may not faile . . .

but the end is gone.

The leaf to which f. 111 is pasted is a bit of an account roll on vellum (xv) beginning :   Summa   ccxv

(?) E quibus adiunctis supra cum cignis xlviij.   In decima solut.

Priori de Heryngham . . . (cut)

I Rectori eccl. de Bury et Vicario de Amberle, etc.

Mention of Ioh. Kyng de Gretham.   Villani Arundell—Hospicium domini—Hospicium domine Marga(rete).

Heringham was a priory in Sussex, and to that region the accounts refer.

GUILLAUME DE MACHAUT.

C.M.A. vac.   **[1594.]**

Vellum, 8⅕ × 6, ff. 44, double columns of 32 lines.   Cent. xv.   Well written, in rather a current hand : brown ink.   2 f. Qui mi donnerent.

Collation : 1¹⁰–3¹⁰ 4⁸ 5⁶.

There is an erasure at top of f. 1 : perhaps Matthaei   C.a.r.d . . .

1. Poem on the Art of Love, The *Remède d'Amour* of Guill. de Machaut, to be edited for the Soc. des anciens textes français by M. Hoepfner.   [1

1. Cilz qui voet aucun art aprendre

A . xii . choses doit entendre

La premiere est q^e doit eslire

Celui ou ses cuers mielx se tire.

Passages of it are set to music, which is described by Mr. Barclay Squire.

On f. 12^b, at the bottom of col. 2, is an oblong miniature : it has gold ground and sprays of gold leaves springing from the angles. It represents on *l.* the façade of a building with door and two turrets : a lady with long flowing hair seated speaking to a youth who reclines on one elbow with his head towards her. He is in a pink robe and apparently tonsured. There are two trees in the background. The execution is not very good.

The text continues on 13^a :

Et quant a p*ar* moi debatus
Me fu assez et combatus
Et fait ma plainte et ma clamour etc.

On 17^b sqq. is a dialogue between *Lamant* and *Esperance*: on 31 sqq. between *Lamant* and *La dame*.

The poem ends f. 36^b. In the penultimate paragraph the author gives a clue to his name.

Mas en la fin de ce traitie
Que jai compile et traictie
Vueil mon nom et mon surnom mettre
Senz oblier sillabe ne lettre
Et cilz qui sauoir le volra
De legier sauoir le porra
Quar le q*u*art ver si co*m* ie fin
Commencement moien et fin
Et de mon nom qⁱ tous entiers
Y est senz faillir q*u*art ne tiers
Mas il ne conuient adiouster
En ce quart ver lettre ne oster
Quar qui riens y adiousteroit
Mon nom iamas ne trouueroit
Qui ny eust ou plux ou mains
Et pour ce que ie sui es mains
De loyal amour q̄ jaim si
Li fas homage et dis ainsi
Bonne amour je te fas homage
De mains de bouche et de corage
Com cez liges sers redeuables
Fins· loyaulz secrez et estables
Et met cuer corps ame et vigour
Desir penser plaisance et honour
Du tout en toi avec mon viure
Com cilz qui vueil morir et viure
En ton seruice senz retraire
Et certes ie le doi b*ie*n faire
Quant tu me donnez tel espoir
Et que ma douce dame chiere
De bon cuer et a lye chiere
Verra ce dit quai mis a rime
Comment quassez moement/nicement rime
Et cel espoir qui en moi maint
Quencor ma chiere dame me aint
Mon cuer si doucement resioie
Quen grant secret et en grant joie
¹Li change mal u tu me dis
Que pris en gre sera mez dis
Or doint Dieus que bon gre le prengne
Et quen li seruant ne mesprengne.
Amen

¹ "Le 4ᵉ vers de la fin" says Prof. Arthur Piaget of Neuchâtel, " donne quelque chose comme *Guillinmes* (?) *de Machaut*."

2. Tract on Love.   37

Hugue de saint Victor dit ou liure que len appelle Arraste poᵣce que
nulz ne poet rime senz amour.   Et que amours est la vie de lame et
vraiement il dit voir · car amours est la vie de lame le confort du cuer ·
la plaisance et le delit du corps.   Et pour tant biaulz signeurs vous deuez
sauoir que il est · iij · Amours.   Vne mercheande · Vne villainne · et vne
loyal bonne et certainne.

Ends f. 43ᵃ: Par foy sire ce dit raisons · vous estez sagez sur tous · et
si narez plux mon fors li beneureuz damours · alez par tout ou vouz
vouldrez quar vous arez bien a plante.   Et je pri amours qui vous gart
et vous en doint trez bonne part.   Amen.

On 44ᵇ is a pencil-sketch of a lady in sixteenth-century (?) costume,
not wholly unskilful.

OCTATEUCH IN ENGLISH.
       C.M.A. 6752. 33.   [1603.]

Vellum, 8$\frac{1}{10}$ × 5$\frac{1}{2}$, ff. 333, double columns of 31 lines.   Cent. xv (about
1430).   Very well written.

The binding and goffring of the fore-edges is exactly uniform with that
of nos. 15, 16, and very beautiful.   A good many leaves have been
supplied in extremely clever facsimile.

Collation: 1⁸ (1 replaced by two leaves) 2⁸–9⁸ (1 replaced) 10⁸ (6 replaced) 11⁸ (8 canc.) 12⁸–16⁸ (1 replaced by two leaves) 17⁸–20⁸ (8 replaced)
21⁸–26⁸ 27⁶ (3 replaced) 28⁸–33⁸ (8 canc.) 34⁸ 35⁸ (5–7 replaced) 36⁸–41⁸
(7 replaced: wants 8).

On f. 1ᵃ is a very elaborate ornamental title with minutely dotted
ground and an ornament in red and blue, most carefully done.   In the
centre of it the words *The Bible* are written in very good Lombardic
capitals of red and blue filled with ornament.

The first leaf is in facsimile and has an initial by the same hand as the
title: in fact I do not doubt that all the facsimile work is by this same
hand, and I should conjecture, from the style, that in some cases at least
the original leaves were preserved, though perhaps in a mutilated and
dirty condition.   It is not likely, for instance, that a seventeenth-century
writer would have invented the title at the beginning of Genesis which
exactly suits this particular manuscript.

Possibly investigation among Pepys' calligraphic collection would reveal
the identity of the writer, who must have been one of the most skilful of
his time.

Contents.   The Octateuch in the more recent Wycliffite version.
No. 123 in Forshall and Madden's list.

Genesis. 2

Rubric.—Here biginneþ þe bible playnly þe text and where þat ony maner clause is set in þe text and is not þerof · lire (i. e. Nicholas de Lyra) certifieþ it plainly.

There are in fact a number of references to *lire* in the margin.

Exodus. First leaf in facsimile. 66

f. 79. Exod. xi–xii also in facsimile.

f. 121. End of Exodus in facsimile. 121ᵇ blank.

Leviticus. First leaf in facsimile. 122

f. 161. End of Leviticus in facsimile. 161ᵇ blank.

Numbers. The initial (original) is in blue with red flourishing. 162

f. 212. Num. xxxiii–xxxiv in facsimile.

Deuteronomy. 216

Joshua : with prologue. At þe last whanne þe · v · bookis of moises weren eendid (= Tandem finito Pentateucho). 263

ff. 275–7 on Jos. ix–xi in facsimile.

Judges. 296

Ruth. 329

f. 333. Ruth iv (part) in facsimile.

Colophon : This is þe eend.

Followed by a heart-shaped piece of ornament.

JEAN MALLART.

      C.M.A. vac.   [1607.]

Vellum, $8\frac{3}{10} \times 6\frac{2}{5}$, ff. 24, 16 and 12 lines to a page. Cent. xvi. In a fine Roman hand; written by Jean Mallart.

Binding : green velvet.

Collation : 1^6 (1 lining cover ; + 2 after 1) $2^4\ 3^2$–$5^2\ 6^4\ 7^2$.

1. A tres illustre tres noble et tres excellent seigneur Monsʳ Henry Kneuet cheuallier et lung de la chambre priuee du Roy.

Canticque panegeric.   2

> Or ha celluy qui tant d'honneur acquiert
> Tire mon cueur, et mon esprit d'esmoy
> Or a celluy que tout chacun requiert
> Tant poursuyuy, que seruiray le Roy
>
> Car si le pere en l'admeralite
> Acquist dhonneur autant comme pompee
> Le filz est ia Attulle en verite, etc.

Ends :

> Celluy qui quiert au plaisir des meduses
> Seruir au Roy dung orateur Francoys
>   Fin.

Iehan mallart orateur et escripuain.

2. Le Cantique de tristesse que ledit orateur a presente a la maieste du Roy. [3^b

A grenouys (Greenwich ?)

Canticque 4

> Comment pourray ie en une terre estrange
> Chanter doulx vers veu que suys en la fange
> Tout incertain sil fault qu'encor ie change
> En aultre terre
> Voela de quoy deuant sa noble grace
> En attendant ie chante et psalmodie.

Ends:

> Tant la douleur qui me poursuyt et chasse 8^b
> Que sa vertu qui passe melodie. 9

It is possible that leaves are gone between 8^b and 9, yet the rhyme fits.

Fin
I. mallart orateur et escripuain.

3. Priere a dieu pour la prosperite des Roys tiree de la philosophie en forme de paraphrase harmonicque sus la patenostre presentee audit S^r a Hentoncourt (= Hampton Court). 9
Compose par le dict mallart poete et Escripuain.

Pater noster. 10

> Pere eternel de qui toute nature
> Deppend et uent et toute creature.

This portion of the book is illustrated by woodcuts measuring 82 × 53 mm. printed on pages otherwise blank, viz. ff. 9^b, 11^b, 12^b, etc. to 16^b.

They represent. 1. Above, the Father half length in clouds in tiara with sword and orb. Before Him the dove, below this IHS.: below, a group of people kneeling on earth with upraised hands.

2. *Adveniat.* Pentecost. The Virgin seated. Apostles sit, stand, and kneel, all with flames on their heads. The dove in glory above.

3. *Fiat voluntas tua,* etc. The Father above in tiara with orb, blessing. Below, Christ crowned with thorns bearing the cross to *r.*, followed by a number of people also bearing crosses.

4. *Panem nostrum.* Paul on steps addressing people on *l.*, and pointing to a scene of the gathering of the Manna, above their heads.

5. *Et dimitte.* In a vaulted prison, Christ on *l.*, three prisoners and a gaoler carrying chains and keys. None of the prisoners are fettered, but part of a pair of bolts lies in the foreground.

6. *Et ne nos.* Job on his dunghill: a devil on *l.* behind him, his wife on *r.*, ruined house on *l.*, and the Father in the sky.

7. *Sed libera.* In a room, a dying man on a bed: a woman kneels with a taper: three other figures. Christ at the foot of the bed on *r.*

The last two cuts have the signature IF.

The poem ends:

> Nons te prions par ta grace assouuye
> Donner aux Roys tressaine et longue vie.
> Amen.

17ᵇ, 18ᵃ blank.

4. Alia Paraphrastica in precationem dominicam Elegia Authore d.
Ioanne Mal(lart). 18ᵇ

Pater noster.

> O ingens bonitas tam blando nomine qui te
> Vis compellari si qua rogandus eris.

Ends 23ᵇ:

> Laeta sit ut nobis atque omine fausta secundo
> Tam sancti voti sancta coronis · amen.

f. 24 blank.

A John Mallard "orator, in the French tongue," appears in Henry VIII's
payments in 1540–1; nos. 380 and 1489 (in *Letters and Papers*, vol. xvii),
but in no other years. MS. Bodl. 883 (3076) is another poem by
Mallart.

MEDICA.

C.M.A. 6800. 81. [1661.]

Vellum, 8⅜ × 5½, ff. 176, 30 and 33 lines to a page. Cent. xiv. In
several hands, one of which is specially fine.

Collation: 1⁸ 2⁸ (+1) | 3⁸ 4⁸ 5⁸ (wants 3–6) 6⁸ 7⁸ 8² 9¹² 10⁸–14⁸ | 15⁸
16⁸ | 17⁸–21⁸ | 22 (four: a gap before 4th) 23¹⁰ (wants 10).

A useful list of contents by Dr. Waterland is on the fly-leaf.

A name obliterated is at top of p. 1.

1. A gode medicyne for to don awey ache & brussode blood. 1

2. Here begynneth þe tresour of poure men. 1
A medycyne for þe ston and ache of þe reynes.
Charms are crossed out on pp. 15, 16, 29.

pp. 22–7 treat of urines; on 28 are notes of the temperaments,
elements, and seasons.

Ends with a section on planets, signs, and divisions of time.

—the morwe sterre he is þe most bryghtest sterre of heuene.

This cannot be a complete text of the *Thesaurus pauperum* (the original
of which is attributed to Petrus Hispanus = John xx or xxi). The copies
of the English version seem to vary considerably.

3. In a very good large hand.
Surgery of Theodoric and Lanfranc. 35
To my worscheppeful fadir and ffrende worthieste and most honourable
man syre archebyschop of valentyne. ffrere theodorys thow vnworthy
I bygynne a werk of surgerye. Sum tyme worthy fader we boþe beyng
togeder at rome, etc. — Departe we on · iiij · partyes þˢ book yᵗ ordeyned
by hys owne capetris to þe furst partye of þis book.

Capitula in red (18).   p. 38 blank.   37
Text.   The causes of woundes solucioun buþ twey generale.
Lib. II—Prol. Ihesu cryst of hefne myn lodeman of þe disputyng of
woundes sores olde and nywe, etc.   66
Capitula (15) written in part twice, as it seems, on pp. 66 and 67.
Four leaves are wanting after p. 70, carrying away the end of Cap. III
and Capp. IV–XV except a few lines.
Lib. III.   We haue sayd of dislocacioun of bones noȝt fulliche, etc. 71
Capitula (37).   71
The festre is an olde depe wounde strayte wᵗ knottynesse, etc.
pp. 71 to 78 near the end are by another hand ; then a very fine hand
begins.
p. 107 with the text of Cap. XV (so numbered: perhaps 10 in the
Capitula) is mutilated : the verso blank; another leaf with blank recto is
then inserted and the text of Cap. XV repeated, on the verso, by the same
scribe.   The text is continued on p. 109 by another hand.
The text of this third book does not agree with the Capitula.   There is
more in the text than in the Capitula and the order is disturbed.
Quire 9, pp. 109–32, is by one hand; p. 132 is blank.   Quire 10 is
in a very good hand resembling that of quire 7, etc., but smaller.
Quire 9 has matter corresponding to Capp. VII, XII, XIII, with other
matter, about dislocations, etc.
Quires 10, etc., have Capp. XIV–XXXVII with additions, chiefly con-
cerning the eyes: ending *Of the palsie & the cure of hym.*
The last words are : and the oignements byneþe.   Explicit tho theodorik
etcetera and lankfrank.
Then follows : A confection of Theodorik and other receipts.   198
p. 212 blank.   Another hand follows.
4. On unguents.   Unguentum for impetigo and serpigo.   213
These be þe perilous dayes in þe ȝer.   229
Further receipts.   230
Change of hand on p. 235.
Sol þe sunne is noblest of alle planetis.   A short tract on the year
in which occur the words (p. 236): verbi gratia we arn now in
m. ccc. lxxxxij ȝere of crist.
Ends p. 240.
pp. 241–4 blank: a writer in the sixteenth century intended to make
a table of the medicines, but has written only the heading.
5. Another hand.
Alphabetical list of materia medica.   245
Alleluya panis cuculi payn de cukulle wodesowre stubwort
Ending : zizannia nigella gith lollium cockell.

6. Here begynneþ medecines gode for diuers euelys on mennes bodys be callen erchebysschopes auicenna and ypocras j coupoñ (? Cophon) ie de and on (*sic*) hole materie aȝen brouȝt and ferst of herbis. 266
Rewe is hot and dreyȝe, etc.
Various simples are described. After the ' vertues of rose maryne ' follows a series of sections in verse written as prose.
,*Betonica of herbis · xxvi · xxiiijti.* I wil ȝou tellyn by & bi. As y fond wretyn in a book · þat in borwyng y be took · Of a gret ladyes prest · þat of gret name þe mest. 288
The other sections are on Centaurea, Solsequium, Celidonia, Pipenella, Materfemia, Ueruena, Mortagon, Peruinca, Rosa, Lilium, Jusquiamus, Affodillue, Dragaunce, Aristologi, Baldemoyne, Egrimonye.
This ends imperfectly with p. 308.
p. 309, etc., quire 21, is in prose, chiefly on the manufacture of aqua vitae and oils; ending p. 324.

7. A smaller hand, which varies in the course of the quire.
Receipts:

On p. 333. (I)on paulyn wan þᵗ y was in þe syȝth of alizaunde & loked þer on a certeyn bok salus vite hellþe of lyf þᵗ boke made aleyn þe phylisophere & wrot þer ine þyngys þᵗ ben verray & trewe as he tellyt in þᵗ same bok & tranlatyd þᵗ same bok owt of grw in to latyn þerine I fond xii experimentys þᵗ foluyn here.
Again on p. 335. ffor soþᵉ I Jon paulyn aue asayd many of þese & y aue fowndyn hem trewe etc.

Other receipts follow, ending on p. 349.
Here and at various other places in the book a name is written (xvi) which looks like Peter Codoy or Codñn.
Also: Gilbert Shephard, p. 349.
On 350 are faint old scribbles.

KALENDAR.
C.M.A. vac. [1662.]

Vellum: in a cuir bouilli case of an oblong form tapering at the top almost to a point, and open at top and bottom. The extreme length is 8½ in., breadth 3 in.
The case is covered with a very pretty pattern of foliage, incised.
It was evidently intended to be hung at the girdle.
The manuscript in it is of similar form to the case, tapering to a point at the top where there is a loop of yellow silk (?) which passed through the hole at the top of the case.

It consists of ten sheets, the shape of which when unfolded is as below:

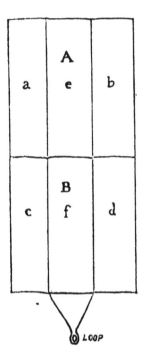

The upper half A folds down over B and the lateral divisions, *a b c d* fold over the central one *e f.*

In some cases the sheet is of only half the size, consisting of portion B.

The majority of the sheets are blank on half of the outer side, save for an endorsement.

The date of the manuscript is early in cent. xv.

The writing and ornaments are of excellent English style. Its provenance, Durham or the neighbourhood.

Among a fair number of surviving specimens of this type of kalendar, MS. Ashmole 6 seems to be similar in general form but has no case. MS. Lambeth 873, also without case, is similar; it comes from Croyland.

I will take the sheets in order, beginning with the outermost, and describe their contents.

1. Half the full size : recto blank : two columns of writing on the verso. Portions of this are in blacker ink than the main body of the MS., but the hand might well be the same.

Col. 1.   Notes of historical events.

Bellum de Oterborn commissum fuit die mercurii in festo S. Oswaldi, A. d. 1338.
Bellum de Homildon commissum fuit die iouis in exaltacionis S. Crucis, A. d. 1402.
Bellum de Schroweberi commissum fuit die sabati in vig. S. M. Magdalene, A. 1403.
Decollacio Ricardi Archiep. Ebor. in festo S. Willelmi ep. Ebor. litt. dominicali D. a° 1405to.
Blacker ink.   Bellum de agincowrte actum fuit die veneris in festo SS. crispini et crispiniani, A. d. 1415.
Anno do! capta est urbs calisii per edwardum tercium regem anglie, A° 1347.
Transitus Ricardi 2^i regis anglie in scociam, A. d. 1345 (!).
Data incarnacionis Christi fuit ab origine mundi 5199.
Aduentus anglorum in angliam, A° 596.
Aduentus normannorum et conquestus anglie, A. d. 1066.
Martirium S. Oswaldi.
Ab origine mundi, A° 6657.
Transitus S. Cuthberti.
(Martyrdom of St. Thomas of Canterbury erased except the date), A° 1170.
Translacio eiusdem A° 1220.
Interdictum anglie A° 1209.
Relaxacio eiusdem A° 1213.

Bellum Dunelm. A° 1346.
Prima pestilencia, A° 1349.
S. Cuthbertus transfertur dunellmum, A. d. 991.
Sedes episcopales (!) apud cestriam restauratur, A. d. 854.
Coronacio henrici 4⁺ᵗˡ, A° 1399.
Coronacio henrici 5⁺ᵗˡ, A° 1413.

Col. 2. Distances from the earth to the several planets and firmament, ending :

Sunt itaque a terra usque ad celum mill' c. mill' ix milia et 3. c. 75 miliaria (? 1109375).

List of kings of England with lengths of reigns from William I to 'Henricus 6ᵗᵘˢ. 39 annis'. This last is probably a later addition.

In Anglia sunt ecclesie paroch. 45 mˡ.
It. feoda militum. 60 mˡ (lined through).
It. sunt ville in anglia. 52 mˡ 80.
It. feoda militum. 60 mˡ. 2 C. 15.
de quibus in manu religiosorum sunt 25 mˡ. 15.

Col. 3 blank.

2. Endorsement. Canon cum tabula festorum mobilium.

Preface to the Table occupying 3 columns on the recto and 2 on the verso with handsome initial in gold with ground of red and blue, patterned with white.

Ad noticiam tabularum kalendarii sequencium. Primo ponitur tabula docens legere algorismum.

It gives a list of almost the whole contents of the MS. ending

—figure eclipsium quarum canones cum ipsis repertis in suis locis et cetera. Expl.

In speaking of the second table on this sheet, it is said : 'Incipit ciclus primus anno domini 1463 et finitur ultimus A.d. 1539'. But in both cases the dates have been altered.

The Tables themselves are thus entitled :

a. Tabula docens legere algorismum per numerum latinum. Et quia numeri in latino non excedunt sexaginta. ultra illam summam non est protensa.
The Arabic numerals are in red and are rather faint.

b. Tabula docens pro · 140 · annis ab A. d. 1367. quis sit annus bisextilis que litera dominicalis et que primacio inchoando annum a circumcisione domini excepta indictione que renouatur octauo Kalendas octobris.

Sheets 3 to 6 contain the Kalendar. Each is endorsed with the names of three of the months. On each the first month occupies half the recto and the two others the verso. Each month has the feasts etc. in the central columns, the side columns giving tables of coniunctiones, cicli, ortus solis, locus planetarius etc. The KL at top of each month is in massive gold on ground of red and blue with white lines.

D

The entries of feasts are in black, scarlet (*s*), crimson (*c*), and gold.

Jan.   9. Deduccio Christi in Egiptum.   *s.*
      12. Benedicti in Were (i. e. Benedict Biscop).
Feb.   10. Scolastice V.   *c.*
      15. Diabolus a domino recessit.   *s.*
Mar. 18. Edwardi regis.   *s.*
      20. Deposicio b. Cuthberti.   *c.*
Apr.   11. Guthlaci presb.
      19. Alphegi ep.
      24. Wlfridi ep. 111.
May   7. Iohannis archiep.   *c.*
      9. Trans. Nicholai.
      19. Dunstani archiep.   *s.*
      21. Godrici heremite.   com.
      26. Augustini ep.   *s.*   Bede.
      27. Commemoracio bede presb.   *b.*
June   8. Willelmi archiep.   *c.*
      17. Botulfi.
      22. Albani prothom.   d.   *s.*
      23. Etheldrede V.
July   4. Ordinacio martini.   t'.
      7. Transl. thome m.   *s.*
      11. Transl. s. benedicti *in gold* with octave in crimson.
      15. Tr. swithuni ep.   *s.*
      26. Anne.   *s.*
Aug.   5. Osuualdi regis *in gold* with octave in black.
      20. Osuuini reg. et m.   *s.*
      25. Ebbe V.   *s.*
      28. Augustini doctoris.   *c.*
      31. Aedani ep. et reliquiarum.   *s.*
Sept.   3. Ordinacio gregorii pape.   *c.*
      4. S. Cuthberti Ep., *in gold*, with octave in scarlet.
      24. Concepcio S. Joh. bapt.
Oct.   2. Thome herford.   d.   *s.*
      10. Paulini ep.   iii lc.
      12. Wilfridi ep.   d.   *s.*
      13. Edwardi reg.   *s.*
      14. Kalixti pape *black.*   bellum an*glorum* (?).   *s.*   (i.e. Hastings.)
      17. Etheldrede V.   *s.*
      19. ffrideswide V.   *s.*
      23. S. romani archiep.   *s.*
Nov. 16. Edmundi archiep.   *s.*
      17. Hilde V.
      20. Edmundi R. et m.   *s.*
Dec.   4. Leonarde abb.   *c.*   Erroneously repeated from Nov. 4.

The northern and especially the Durham saints are prominent in this Kalendar.

7. Endorsed: Tabula planetarum cum canone. Tabula lune. Imago signorum.

There is also a circular diagram in red much effaced.

This sheet is (like 1) only half the size: the upper half has been lost.

One column of writing remains on the outer side beginning imperfectly : quodlibet immediate sequitur signum fixum et signum commune. and ending: sed aquosa (?) per lineam croceam subtractam (?) a terreis discernuntur.

Within is a very good picture of this form with gold frame, and ground

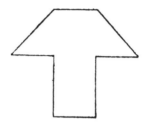

divided quarterly into red and blue, patterned with lines and dots in black, white, and red.

The subject is the influence of the zodiacal signs upon various parts of the human body; this is represented (as usual) by a human figure with the signs perched about upon the different organs. The figure here is that of a nude youth with yellow hair, well drawn. His arms are extended.

The text begins: *Aries*. Caue ab inscisione in capite uel in facie et ne inscindas uenam capitulem,

and ends: *Pisces*. Caue ne inscindaris in pedibus.

8. Endorsed: Eclipses lune.

A table of eclipses, figured in the usual manner, for the years 1429 to 1462. Twenty-eight figures are given.

Then follows what may be the beginning of another table.

Prima pars dicit quantum eclipsabitur de diametro corporis. Secunda enarrat tempus casus. Tercia dicit dimidium more. Quarta duracionem totalem eclipsis in tempore.

Two figures only follow.

9. Endorsed: Tabula pro fleobotomia.

Text (with large gold initial) in three columns on the outer side.

Minucio fit alia per methatesim alia per antifrasim

Ending on col. 1 of the upper half of the inner side: digito postea subtracto subito cum impetu exit sanguis. Amen. Explicit.

Cols. 2, 3 are blank.

The lower half of the inner side is occupied by a circular diagram, containing a nude human figure, beautifully drawn in outline, with red lines proceeding from various veins in his body to medallions arranged around: in these medallions are legends of this form : Uena iuxta nares incisa purgat caput auditum iuuat et confortat.   There are twenty of these.

10. No visible endorsement.   This sheet is half the size of the rest, but apparently complete.   The outer side is blank.   The inner contains :
    Tabula de iudiciis urinarum per colores.

It consists of a large circle round which are arranged twenty vessels to illustrate the colours.   Explanatory text is written outside them.

MUSICA.
        C.M.A. 6806. 87.   [1760.]

Vellum, $8\frac{4}{5} \times 5\frac{9}{10}$, ff. 3 + 88 + 2 free, 8 lines of music and words to a page. Cent. xv late or xvi early.   Very well written in Roman hand: Flemish.

The binding has been of cloth of gold (over paper boards) of which the relics remain: it has been rebacked for Pepys and lettered: K. Hen. 7. Musick.   On the flyleaf in an old hand is: no. 1281 (or 7).   The writing of this indicates that the book was once in the Royal Library.

Collation: a^4 (1 lining cover) 1^8–11^8 b^4 (wants 3 : 4 lining cover).

Inside the cover is written (xvi) :
1 · 13 · 13 · 5 · 18 · 19 · 1 · 13 · 8 · 14 · 15 ·:·
9 · 18 · 12 · 9 · 8 · 14 · 15 · 5 ·:·
i.e. Anne Stanhop
        is mi hope.
and : he that stelle thys boke a shalle be
hangked vp on a hoke nouther be watter nor
be lond bot wyt a fayer hempyng bond.
ff. ii, iii a blank.

On iii^b at top a panel of ornament: ground vertical bands of green and white.   The arms of Henry VII surmounted by a crown and surrounded with the garter and motto: supporters; red dragon and white hound collared.

Below.   In laudem celestis regine.
        Tabula huius codicis.
List of the songs in the book, ending
Finis Tabulae.
f. iv blank.

f. i has writing on the recto: but the important side was the verso which is bordered and has had a picture about half-page.   This has been cut out.

There is also a border to f. ii^a. Both are of dead gold with naturalistic flowers, fruits, and insects. In the lower margin of each is a shield *argent*, a cross engrailed *gules*: this is surmounted in each case by a cross fleury outlined on the gold ground of the border and erased.

Each piece of music in the volume has an initial on fluid gold, or coloured, ground. These, and the other ornaments, are very well executed. They are by a foreign hand, or at least one trained in a foreign school.

The picture which has been cut out may, I fear, have disappeared since Pepys' time. This I infer from the description of the MS. in the *Cat. MSS. Angl.* of 1697:

6806. 87. Vocal Musick (of different styles) compos'd by the most Eminent Masters, English and Forrein, in the time of King Hen. VII for the then Prince of Wales; being the Prince's Original Book, elegantly prickt and *illuminated with his Figure in Miniature*. Pergam.

In the last cover is written (xvi)

For my lady anne ... (? stanhop: but it does not look much like the name).

The Table of Contents as transcribed by Mr. Barclay Squire runs as follows:

Tabula huius Codicis		f. 2^b–3^b
1. Ave Maria. Canon (4 voc.). Mutilated. Jo. Bortel.		f. i
2. Que est ista. Canon (4 voc.). Mutilated. Antoine de Fevin.		f. i
3. Ista est speciosa. Canon (4 voc.). Mathieu Gascogne.		f. i^b
4. Dulcis amica dei (3 voc.). Jean Prioris.		f. ii
5. Dei genitrix (4 voc.). ,, ,,		f. ii^b
6. Verbum bonum (4 voc.). Pierkin or Pierre de Therache (ascribed in the index to A. de Fevin).		f. iii^b
7. Suscipe verbum (4 voc.). Bontemps.		f. v^b
8. O admirabile commercium (4 voc.). Josquin des Prés.		f. vii^b
9. Quando natus es (4 voc.). ,, ,,		f. ix^b
10. Rubum quem viderat (4 voc.). ,, ,,		f. xi^b
11. Germinavit radix Jesse (4 voc.). ,, ,,		f. xii^b
12. Ecce Maria genuit (4 voc.). ,, ,,		f. xiii^b
13. Ave Maria (4 voc.). Jo. Mouton.		f. xv^b
14. Ecce Maria genuit (4 voc.). Jo. Mouton.		f. xvi^b
15. Sub tuum praesidium (4 voc.). Antoine Brumel.		f. xvii^b
16. Sancta Trinitas unus Deus (4 voc.). A. de Fevin.		f. xix^b
17. Nobilis progenie nobilior fide (4 voc.). A. de Fevin.		f. xxi^b
18. Adiutorium nostrum (4 voc.). ,, ,,		f. xxiii^b
19. Lectio Prima (4 voc.). Robert de Fevin.		f. xxv^b
20. Lectio Secunda (3 voc.). ,, ,,		f. xxviii^b
21. Lectio Tertia (4 voc.). A. de Fevin.		f. xxxi^b

22. Quam pulchra es (4 voc.). Jean Prioris. f. xxxiii^b
23. Benedicite and Agimus tibi gratias (4 voc.). J. Mouton. f. xxxiv^b
24. Sufficiebat nobis paupertas nostra (4 voc.). Jean Richafort. f. xxxvi^b
25. O preclara stella maris (3 voc.). A. de Fevin. f. xxxviii^b
26. Dulcis mater (3 voc.). M. Gascogne. f. xxxix^b
27. Ave Maria (3 voc.). J. Prioris. f. xli^b
28. Inclita pura (3 voc.). A de Fevin. f. xlii^b
29. Nigra sum (3 voc.). M. Gascogne. f. xliii^b
30. Parce Domine (3 voc.). Obreh [Jacob Obrecht]. f. xlvi^b
31. On a mal dit de mon amy (3 voc.). A. de Fevin. f. xlvii^b
32. Tres doulce dame (3 voc.).   „   „ f. xlviii^b
33. Maudits soient ces maris jaloux (3 voc.). A. de Fevin. f. xlix^b
34. Helas je suys marry (3 voc.).   „   „ f. li^b
35. Je le laire puys qui my bat (3 voc.).   „   „ f. lii^b
36. Chacun maudit ces jaleux (3 voc.).   „   „ f. liii^b
37. En amours na sinon (3 voc.).   „   „ f. lv^b
38. Petite Camusette (3 voc., without words).   „   „ f. lvii^b
39. Fors seulement (3 voc.).   „   „ f. lviii^b
40. Il faict bon escouter (3 voc.).   „   „ f. lx^b
41. Jayme bien mon amy (3 voc.). N. le Petit (A. de Fevin in the Index). f. lxii^b
42. Adieu solas tout plaisir (3 voc.). A. de Fevin. f. lxiii^b
43. Faulte dargent cest doleur (3 voc.). A. de Fevin. f. lxiv^b
44. Jay veu la Beauté (3 voc.).   „   „ f. lxv^b
45. Il mest advis (3 voc.). Hyllayre (Perrichon in the Index). f. lxvii^b
46. Dieu gard de mal (3 voc.). J. Mouton. f. lxviii^b
47. Jay mys mon cueur (3 voc.). M. Gascogne. f. lxx^b
48. Je voys je viens (3 voc.).   „ f. lxxii^b
49. Pastourelle dieu (3 voc.).   „ f. lxxiii^b
50. Pour avoir faict (3 voc.).   „ f. lxxiv^b
51. En ce joly temps (3 voc.).   „ f. lxxvi^b
52. Celle qui ma demandé (3 voc.).   „ f. lxxviii^b
53. Helas ma dame que j'ayme (3 voc.). Jo. Brunel. f. lxxix^b
54. N'aymes jamés une villaine (4 voc.). A. de Fevin. f. lxxxi^b
55. D'amours je suys desheritée (5 voc.). J. Richafort. f. lxxxiii^b
56. Si j'eusse Marion (4 voc.). M. Gascogne. f. lxxxiv^b
57. Consommo la vita mya (4 voc.). J. Prioris. f. lxxxvi^b

CORONATION PAGEANT OF QUEEN CLAUDE OF FRANCE.
C.M.A. 6727. 12.   [1791.]

Vellum, 9 × 6, ff. 48, 18 lines to a page. Cent. xvi. In Gothic hand with elaborate but coarse pictures. Stiff vellum wrapper stained green with some gold tooling (xvii): end papers of green and gold.

Collation: 1^2 (1 canc.) 2^8–7^8 (wants 7).

Le sacre couronnement tryumphe et entree de la tres crestienne royne et duchesse ma souueraine dame et maistresse madame Claude fille du trescrestien Roy Loys xii^e de ce nom. Et de madame anne de bretaigne deux foys royne sacree et couronnee en france, etc. etc. et sa reception faicte a paris . . . Et de son Regne Le iii^e.   2

Louenge a dieu pere omnipotent, etc. . . . Parlerons en premier Lieu de sa venue a s^{ct} denis et de son couronnement faict audit lieu Le dimenche x^e Jour de may Lan de grace mil cinq cent dix sept.   2^a

On 6^a the arms of France and Brittany impaled.

The narrative of the coronation and entry ends 48^a:

Et signifians iceulx princes les deulx nobles roys francyon et brutus princes des francoys et bretons Et de qui les deulx principaultes portoit le nom. Ainsy finit cette noble assemblee.

No^{u}s priions dieu et la virge marie quy luy doint fruict bonne et longue vie. Amen.

Claude became queen in 1515 and died in 1524: her husband was Francis I.

The book is illustrated with full-page pictures of what I must call very bad execution: good in colour, but very coarse, and with a quantity of fluid gold. They represent:

1. 1^b. The writer, who has on his arm a stole or amess of the arms of France and Brittany, offering his book (bound in green and gold) to the King throned on *l.*: four courtiers are seen.

2. 16. The Coronation Mass. The legate in red biretta is the celebrant, three bishops assist. The queen and ladies on a platform: a page holds the crown over her head.

3. 30^b. A device shown at the Porte St. Denis, representing: The Queen. The dove bearing a crown down out of a gold cloud. Six women hold labels: Rachel, Rebekah, Esther, Leah, Sarah, Deborah. Below, in black and white habits, Justice, Magnanimity, Prudence, Temperance (without emblems).

4. 32^a. At the *Fontaine du ponceau nommée la fontaine de la Royne*. A gold fountain. In front a salamander and an ermine. At the rim of the fountain the Queen and the two princesses, Louise and Charlote. She holds a golden apple spouting water.

Above: *Rex plantauit ego rigaui(t) deus autem incrementum dedit.*

5. 33^a. At La Trinité. Above, the King and Queen throned. On *l.*, *Prudence* and *Connoissance*. On *r. Bon conseil* with a paper and *Bon voulloir* with a banner. Below: Three figures among lilies. *c., Le peuple francoys* with a mattock. *l., Victoire* with a club. *r., Viuoy* with a club.

6. 34^c. At the Porte aux Peintres. Above: at top, Charity, half-length in rays, below her in *c., Foy* rising out of a flower and holding a banner with the arms of God, the Pope, and the King. On *l.* and *r.*, four females, *Nyade, Amadriade, Oreade, Nappde* (? Nereid or Napaïd—if such there be).

Below in *c.*, a youth half-length, Tantalus, with a vessel whence jets of water spout into gold vessels held by Pope, Cardinal, and Bishops on *l.* Ten peers and three kings on *r.*

7. 36. At the Fontaine de S. Innocent. At top, three crowned shields of France, France impaled with France and Brittany quarterly, and France impaled with *gules*, and cross *argent.*

Under this a large golden heart open, within which are three females, *Amour diuine, A. naturelle, A. coniugalle.*

Below, figures of Abigail kneeling to David with offerings, Julia holding a pax with the figure of the world, Portia swallowing a coal, Veturia showing her breast to Coriolanus.

8. 37ª. At the Châtelet. A tree: the king and queen at top. Princes, kings, and dukes of Brittany on the lower branches. At the foot four females seated: *Seuerite, Coustume, Mansuetude, Loy.*

9. 40°. At the Palais Royal. Above: St. Louis throned: on left stands his mother, and on *r.*, Justice.

Below: Three men, *Le poure, Le laboureur, Lauenturier*, each holding up a letter (a petition).

At bottom: The shields of France, and France impaled with France and Brittany quarterly.

44ª is blank.

10. 48ᵇ. A 'perron' erected at the barrière at the time of the tournament.

At top: The arms of the king and queen under one crown, supported by angels. On the gable, the shields of Monsieur (France with a bordure *gules* supported by lions). Monsᵣ le connestable and M. de Vendôme (each France with bend dexter *gules*: the supporters only varied). Two soldiers with banners of France and Brittany at the angles of the pediment.

A classical façade below, with two arches filled with a ground of ermine: in the one (*l.*) is a horned beast with coloured wings, in the other a hornless beast (? a salamander): both are gold coloured and face to *l.*

APOCALYPSE.

C.M.A. 6764, 45.   [1803.]

Vellum, 9 × 6⅜, ff. 45, varying numbers of lines. Cent. xiv (middle of the century, according to M. Paul Meyer). Well written, by an English hand.

Collation: 1⁸ 2¹⁰ (wants 2) 3¹² (wants 1, 10, 12) 4⁶ (wants 6) 5⁸ (2, 8 canc.) 6⁶ 7⁴ (wants 3, 4).

Lettered by Pepys: Apoc. Vis. MSS.

Contents.

The Apocalypse in Latin accompanied by a rhymed French version.

The Latin text is written in long lines, the French in double columns below it.

The French version has been printed from the seven known MSS. by M. Paul Meyer in *Romania*, xxv, 174 sqq. The copies described and used by him are:

1. Cambridge, Corpus Christi College, no. 20 (from St. Augustine's, Canterbury).
2. The present MS.
3. Copenhagen Royal Library MS. Thott 89 (of English origin).
4. British Museum, Royal 2 D. XIII.
5. British Museum, Add. 18633 (formerly the Earl of Denbigh's).
6. Toulouse MS. 815 (closely resembling the last).
7. Cambridge, Fitzwilliam Museum, McClean MS. 123 (from the Convent of Nuneaton).

All these MSS. are of English origin and were written in the fourteenth century.

No. 7 appears to be as early in date as any. They are divided by M. Meyer into three families.

    I. *a.* consists of nos. 2, 4, 7 of our list.
    II. *β.* no. 3.
    III. *γ.* nos. 1, 5, 6.

The characteristics of *a* are ' 1° que le texte de l'Apocalypse y est traduit presque entièrement; il est très rare qu'un verset soit omis; 2° que les MSS. de ce groupe présentent la même disposition : le haut de chaque page est occupé par une miniature ; au-dessous est écrit le latin ; enfin, sous le latin, sont copiés les vers français.'
    In *β* the text of the first three chapters is much abridged.
    In *γ* besides this abridging of the text there are these further differences ; (1) that a comment in French prose is added; (2) that the miniatures are not confined to the top of the page, but are set irregularly in the text.
    In the copy before us the pictures vary in height from about $2\frac{3}{10}$ to 4 inches. The frames are of blue and pink patterned with white and with squares of gold or ornament at the angles. A portion of the ground is nearly always of burnished gold. The rest will be either red (more than one shade occurs), blue, or brown, patterned. St. John is uniformly bearded : the colours of his mantle and robe vary. He usually stands on *l.* in each picture holding a red or green staff. Angels are robed in white as a rule, and nimbed : their wings are coloured. The execution of the pictures is good, but not of the first class.
    2 D. XIII. resembles this MS. very closely in respect of the composition of the pictures. It is a badly executed book. The pictures are at the tops of the pages; of uniform size, without backgrounds.
    Initials to the text are in gold, either flourished in red or blue, or upon a ground of colour with devices in white.
    The Latin text begins : Apocalipsis ihesu christi quam dedit deus etc.
    The French : La reuelacioun de ihesucrist
            Que dex a ses serfs demustrer fist. (Meyer, p. 187.)

M. Meyer gives only specimens of the text of the α family of MSS. including the beginning and end. Our copy ends thus:

Qui porte tesmoigne de ceo voire
Je viene tost amen vien ihesu sire
La grace de ihesu nostre seingnour
Od nous soit a tot iour. Amen.

The cycle of pictures in this (and other) rhymed Apocalypses conforms, without great exactness, to the scheme which has been so clearly set forth by M. Delisle (*L'Apocalypse en français, Soc. d. anc. textes fr.*): it must be classed with the *second* family of MSS. there described.

The subjects of the pictures are as follows:

1. 1ᵃ. John seated with staff by a tree on an island: water with fishes in front. A rabbit feeding on the island. An angel flying horizontally out of a cloud on *r.* speaks.

2. 1ᵇ. John looks at a walled city containing seven buildings with spires, and one dome (the Seven Churches).

3. 2ᵃ. Christ in *c.* in mandorla edged with clouds: the twelve Apostles kneel on *r.* and *l.* (Behold He cometh with clouds.)

4. 2ᵇ. Christ robed in white with white hair, gold belt, fire-coloured face, sword in mouth, holding a gold disk with seven red balls on it in *r.* hand. Key dependent from *l.* Behind Him an altar, with gold trefoil arcading in front, on which are seven gold candlesticks. John prostrate at His feet, and also, again, on *l.*, beholding Him.

5-11. 3ᵃ-6ᵃ. The Letters to the Seven Churches. In each of these pictures John sits on *l.* writing. In *c.*, a seated Bishop in chasuble or cope, and mitre, with crosier. On *r.*, a church with doorway on *l.*, and steeple or bell cot with two bells: usually there is a clerestory with single or double round-headed windows. In one instance there are quatrefoils.

12. 6ᵇ. Angel leads John to *r.* by the hand. On *r.*, John puts his head through a small double doorway in air surrounded by clouds and surmounted by a gable and pinnacles.

13. 7ᵃ. God on the rainbow in *c.* in mandorla. The lamps hang above Him. The four beasts are in the spandrels. The Elders in white, crowned, in four rows of six each on *r.* and *l.*

14. 7ᵇ. A similar arrangement, a larger picture. The Elders in coloured robes hold or cast down their crowns.

15. 8ᵃ. *l.*, John and Angel (in mantle): the Angel holds a small orb. *c.*, God or Christ (cross-nimbed) in mandorla holds up a sealed book. At His feet a nimbed lion, the Lion of Judah, has the sealed book between his fore paws. *r.*, a nimbed beardless Elder points to the lion and speaks to John.

16. 8ᵇ. Arrangement as in 13. In *c.*, the Lamb with seven horns and eyes on an altar. Blood from His breast flows into a chalice. The Elders (who obviously include the Apostles) are in coloured robes.

17. 9ᵃ. The same arrangement. In *c.*, the Lamb on the knees of God takes the book. The Elders kneel with musical instruments.

18. 9ᵇ. Central mandorla. God blessing. Angels in white on *r.* and *l.* above the Elders who are in two groups only.

A leaf gone.

19. 10ᵃ. The third rider on the black horse. John addressed by Lion's head in cloud.

20. 10ᵇ. The fourth rider. He is of the same dark colour as his horse; he looks back. Behind him is Hell mouth with two brown devils in it. The Eagle in cloud addresses John.

21. 11ᵃ. (*This leaf should follow f.* 12.) *c.*, Four angels stand on a circle in air each holding a human head (a wind). On *r.*, angel holding orb speaks out of fire in cloud.

22. 11ᵇ. Central mandorla. God blessing. Water below. On it two groups each of nine persons, with palms.

23. 12ᵃ. John beardless. Altar with chalice. Nude souls before it (4): one clad by an angel. Bust of Christ in mandorla and cloud.

24. 12ᵇ. Sixth seal. Sun red and moon dark in clouds. Ruined city with heads of dead people below.

25. 13ᵃ. (*This leaf should follow f.* 14.) In red cloud, seven angels (4 and 3) with trumpets : in *c.*, the Lamb in mandorla.

26. 13ᵇ. In red cloud, altar with chalice and smaller chalice-like incense-ship. One angel behind the altar puts incense (in a paper *cornet*?) from this into a censer held by another angel. A third on *r.* holds a red *cornet* (fire?) and a fourth empties the censer upon earth: four red beasts' heads (thunders) pour out flames (viii. 3).

27. 14ᵃ. Central mandorla. God blessing. Water below. On *l.*, eleven people and on *r.*, nine with white stoles about their necks, adoring. Text vii. 11, 12.

28. 14ᵇ. John and Elder with stole who points to group of thirteen people in stoles in white cloud. (vii. 13 sqq.)

29. 15ᵃ. First trumpet. Sun and moon darkened, hail falls, trees uprooted.

30. 15ᵇ. Second trumpet. Sun and moon pale, a mass of fire falls, ship sinks.

31. 16ᵃ. Third trumpet. Red star falls upon four springs and a lake or well.

32. 16ᵇ. Fourth trumpet. Sun, moon, and stars partially darkened.

33. 17ᵃ. Eagle with scroll, *Ve Ve Ve habitantibus terram.* John on *r.*

34. 17ᵇ. Fifth trumpet. (John absent.) Abaddon (or one of the locusts), dark-hued, crowned, with bat's wings, in red surcoat, on horse with red trappings, rides to *r.* Another 'locust' emerges behind him from a cave by which is a star with key dependent from it.

35. 18ᵃ. Four warriors in mail on horses with curious heads, vomiting fire, and serpent-tails, ride to *r.*

36. 18ᵇ. The great angel with sun-face partly concealed by rainbow : one foot on rock in *c.* in sea.

37. 19ᵃ. John at desk. Angel in cloud hands him a pen. In cloud seven red heads of beasts (thunders).

x. 8–xi. 2 *is omitted here.*

38. 19ᵇ. The two witnesses, nimbed, in brown robes covered with hatched lines. They address three persons also nimbed. On *r.* they vomit fire upon three armed men seated on the ground.

39. 20ᵃ. Antichrist: the beast, human, but with hooked nose, beard, lion-hands, and cock's feet, sits crowned on a rock on *l.*, in a green tunic, cross-legged. He is drawing a sword which he holds across his knee, and looks to *r.*

On *r.* he or another, this time in orange red, with bat's wings, stands smiting with sword the two witnesses, who lie on their backs with joined hands.

40. 20ᵇ. The witnesses lying dead. Two doves enter their mouths (the spirit of life). An angel speaks out of a cloud. Above, their feet are seen, ascending in cloud. On *r.*, city falling, hail descending, beasts' heads (thunders) in cloud.

41. 21ᵃ. The seventh trumpet. On *r.*, mandorla with God in it. Five heads of angels in cloud on *l.*, four on *r.* Below, six adoring elders.

42. 21ᵇ. Central mandorla, with God. Below, on *l.* five elders and on *r.* five elders kneel. Thrones (green and red) on *r.* and *l.* (xi. 16).

43. 22ª. The Temple on a cloud in air. It is a steepled and pinnacled church with open trefoiled arch on one side showing altar with a crown on it. Below it, thunders. On earth, fallen city with heads of dead people (xi. 19).

44. 22ᵇ. The woman throned, full face, with nimbus of stars, a white disk behind her: surrounded by flame, and this by clouds. The crescent beneath her feet.

45. 23ª. *l.*, the dragon, vermilion. The woman in a white starred cloud surrounded by flame, hands the child (swaddled) to an angel. The feet of Christ in mandorla. On *r.*, the back of a disappearing figure.

46. 23ᵇ. Three angels (Michael in *c.*) spearing the great dragon and two smaller ones.

47. 24ᵃ. Angel in cloud shows blank scroll to John. The dragon on *r.* faces *l.* (xii. 10).

48. 24ᵇ. The dragon on *l.* Angel in cloud adjusts two wings on the shoulders of the woman who stands between trees on *r.*

49. 25ª. The dragon vomits water into a round black hole. The woman winged, horizontal, in cloud.

50. 25ᵇ. Five warriors (two on *l.*, three on *r.*) in mail, standing on rocks, fight the dragon, in *c.*

A leaf is lost here.

51. 26ª. The Beast, a nude human figure, with clawed feet and with seven lion-like heads and crowned horns, throned, cross-legged with sword. Kneeling figures on *l.* adore him. Kneeling figures on *r*, back to him, adore Christ in mandorla above (xiii. 4).

52. 26ᵇ. The Beast on four legs holding a sword on *r.* fore paw tramples on, kills, and fights the faithful : some of these are in mail with red-cross shields.

53. 27ª. John looks at the Lamb on mount Sion (with cross). Kneeling figures nimbed in two rows adore.

With this leaf the hand changes to one more upright and narrow.

54. 27ᵇ. In air a square frame with central mandorla and the beasts in the spandrels. *r.* and *l.*, clouds, whence come six angels playing harps. On earth below, four nimbed figures (two *r.*, two *l.*) and John (*r.*).

55. 28ª. Six people seated on green mountain. A half-length angel in cloud holds an open book (the Gospel).

56. 28ᵇ. John. Angel in cloud speaking. Ruined city below, with heads of a king and another.

57. 29ª. *l.*, the image of the beast, upright, dark-coloured, holding sword, standing on a green base. *c.*, below, Hell-mouth with souls in it. Above, a cloud : in it the Lamb, six heads of angels *r.* and *l.*, and an angel on *r.* speaking to John (xv. 9).

58. 29ᵇ. John at desk : angel in cloud gives him a pen and points to a mailed warrior who is beheading a kneeling man. Five wounded corpses lie on *r.* (xv. 13, Beati mortui, etc.)

59. 30ª. John. In cloud in air a crowned man with sickle, a sheaf below and standing corn ; some of it is cut and a sickle is there. Above them on *r.*, an angel in cloud, in which the Temple is seen, speaks to the crowned man.

60. 30ᵇ. Above on *l.*, the cloud with the Temple : an angel holding a bill-hook points down. Below is a city and a tree with a bill-hook in the trunk. Across the front is a flood of water streaked with red. Corpses lie in it, and on *r.* two horses advance through it. Above them a cloud with the temple in it showing altar and chalice ; an angel in it, holding a vessel of fire, speaks to the angel on *l.*

61. 31ª. John. In a cloud, seven angels holding the vials, round-bodied bottles with necks.

62. 31^b. John. Green sea with flames in it. Seven white-robed and nimbed harpers stand in it. Above, the Lamb in mandorla and cloud (xv. 2).

A leaf is lost here.

63. 32^a. John. Angel on rock pours the second vial into the sea, a ship sinks (xvi. 3).

64. 32^b. John. The third vial. Angel on rock pours it into water. The angel of the waters in air on *r.* speaks. God above in mandorla in cloud.

65. 33^a. John. The fourth vial. Angel pours it into the sun in a cloud. Flames fall on a group of struggling men below.

66. 33^b. John beardless. The fifth vial poured upon the seat (wooden and four legged) of the beast. His worshippers on *r.* sit and bite their tongues. The background is red streaked with black.

67. 34^a. The sixth vial poured into Euphrates. Angel on rock on *l.* John on rock on *r.*

68. 34^b. John. The dragon (*l.*). The false prophet, upright, dark hued, with ram's head and cloven hoofs for hands and feet, and green loin-cloth. The beast emerging on all-fours from a hole in the ground. All three vomit frogs.

69. 35^a. John beardless. The seventh vial poured on to the blue air. On *r.*, below, fallen city; above, the temple in a cloud, an angel pointing down, and six beasts' heads (thunders).

70. 35^b. Angel leading John. On *r.*, the woman in blue holding a wand, seated. Below her feet and before her are three green rivers (xvii. 1).

71. 36^a. John. The woman, holding a gold cup, on the back of the beast. She is in pink and has white wimple and gold fillet.

72. 36^b. John led by Angel. On *r.*, the woman in blue stooping towards a flagon which is upside down, and spilling its contents. She holds a cup upside down, and is supposed to be drunk (xvii. 6).

There was a dislocation in the archetype at this point: f. 37 illustrates the text of xxi. 1–8 and xx. 11–14^a. f. 38 continues with xviii. 1–xx. 10 which is illustrated on 44^a: 44^b gives us xxii. 6. I shall take the pictures as they are in the book.

73. 37^a. John. Mandorla, with God, in cloud. Church on *r.* with altar and chalice. Et uidi celum nouum *et aerem* et teram nouam, etc. xxi. 1–8.

74. 37^b. John. On *r.*, mandorla with God: a river flows out of it to *l.* between two trees. Et uidi thronum, etc. xx. 11–14^a. The picture illustrates the River of Life xxii. 1 sqq.: and is not the right one for the text.

75. 38^a. John. Fallen city with heads in the ruins. Angel emerges from temple in cloud, holding orb (xviii. 1–3).

76. 38^b. Angel on rock poising a millstone in his hand. *c*, sea with millstone in it. *r.*, John (xviii. 21–24).

77. 39^a. John. Above, central mandorla with beasts in spandrels, and heads of Elders, three on each side ; at the sides of the mandorla six busts of angels blowing trumpets (the text reads, 'audiui, quasi uocem *tubarum* multarum' for 'turbarum'). Below, the woman in pink robe and broad black hat lies on a bed of flames (xix. 1–5).

78. 39^b. John. A table spread, with a fish, etc. on it. Five nimbed men eat and drink. On the nearer side kneels the bride stretching up her hands, holding something, to the Lamb who is on an altar. A half-length angel above holds out a linen cloth in an arch over them. Over this a cloud, out of which an angel blows a trumpet to *l.* (audiui quasi uocem *tube* magne), xix. 6–9^a.

79. 40^a. Bust of Christ in shield-shaped mandorla : angel points to it and addresses John on *l.* *r.*, John kneels to angel who touches his beard and speaks (xix. 9^b–10).

80. 40^b. John. In a cloud, Christ on a dappled horse, holding a book in both

hands; a sword in His mouth; in red robe, followed by mailed warriors on horseback. Below, Christ with sword, treading the winepress (xix. 11–16).

81. 41ᵃ. John. Angel half-length in the sun surrounded by flames and clouds. Below, four ravens perched on corpses of men and beasts (xix. 17, 18).

82. 41ᵇ. In a cloud, Christ with shield on horseback, followed by warriors. His hand is in the attitude of holding a lance, which has not been drawn. On *r.*, the beast on his hind-legs holding a huge scymitar. A warrior beside him (xix. 19).

83. 42ᵃ. Christ with sword, and warriors, in cloud, as before. On earth, two mailed men, with lance and axe, prick the hindquarters of the beast who retreats into a cave in a hill (xix. 20, 21).

84. 42ᵇ. John. Angel in cloud holds the two ends of a chain which is passed round the neck of the red dragon in *c.* On *r.*, an angel puts a key to a brown door (xx. 1–3).

85. 43ᵃ. Three robed men in Jewish caps, throned, each with a sword. Below their feet six nude bodies lie in three's, head to head. On *r.* and *l.* of the man in *c.* are groups of four nude people with joined hands (xx. 4–6).

86. 43ᵇ. *l.*, three mailed men standing, with swords. Then the beast, nude, upright, with sword. A hill, with a little city on the top. In the slope of it a hole out of which the legs and tail of the beast project. Five mailed men lie dead: lions rampant *sable* on two of their shields. In *r.* upper corner, in a cloud, a large bust of Christ (xx. 7–9ᵃ).

87. 44ᵃ. John on *r.* Hell mouth, and in it, the heads of the beast on *l.*, of the false prophet (black, with ram's horns) in *c.*: of the dragon on *r.* (xx. 9ᵇ, 10).

88. 44ᵇ. John. Mandorla in air with Christ throned. *r.*, John kneels to the angel, who touches his beard and points up (xxii. 6–15).

89. 45ᵃ. John. Christ seated in *c.* with orb, between two angels holding candlesticks. He turns to *l.* and touches an open book held by a third angel, which John also touches (xxii. 16–21, end).

f. 45ᵇ is blank.

The following portions of text are given:

f. 1ᵃ. i. 1–3 scripta sunt. quire 1.	f. 10ᵃ. vi. 5, 6.	
1ᵇ. i. 4–6.	10ᵇ. vi. 7, 8.	
2ᵃ. i. 7–11.	11ᵃ. vii. 1–4, omitting 5–8.	
2ᵇ. i. 12–20.	11ᵇ. vii. 9–11ᵃ, quatuor animalium.	
3ᵃ. ii. 1–7.	12ᵃ. vi. 9–11.	
3ᵇ. ii. 8–11.	12ᵇ. vi. 12–17.	
4ᵃ. ii. 12–17.	13ᵃ. viii. 1, 2.	
4ᵇ. ii. 18–29.	13ᵇ. viii. 3–6.	
5ᵃ. iii. 1–6.	14ᵃ. vii. 11ᵇ, 12.	
5ᵇ. iii. 7–13.	14ᵇ. vii. 13–17.	
6ᵃ. iii. 14–22.	15ᵃ. viii. 7.	
6ᵇ. iv. 1. On this page is a paragraph of commentary, Per iiiiᵒʳ animalia intelligitur Christus.	15ᵇ. viii. 8, 9.	
	16ᵃ. viii. 10, 11.	
	16ᵇ. viii. 12.	
7ᵃ. iv. 2–8.	17ᵃ. viii. 13.	
7ᵇ. iv. 9–11.	17ᵇ. ix. 1–6.	
8ᵃ. v. 1–5.	*gap.	
8ᵇ. v. 6, and paragraph of comment.	18ᵃ. ix. 17–21. quire 3.	
9ᵃ. v. 7–10. quire 2.	18ᵇ. x. 1–3ᵃ.	
9ᵇ. v. 11–14, dicebant Amen, and paragraph of comment.	19ᵃ. x. 3ᵇ–7.	
*gap.	*gap in the archetype.	
	19ᵇ. xi. 3–6.	

f. 20ᵃ. xi. 7–10.
20ᵇ. xi. 11–14.
21ᵃ. xi. 15.
21ᵇ. xi. 16–18.
22ᵃ. xi. 19.
22ᵇ. xii. 1, 2.
23ᵃ. xii. 3–6.
23ᵇ. xii. 7–9.
24ᵃ. xii. 10–12.
24ᵇ. xii. 13, 14.
25ᵃ. xii. 15, 16.
25ᵇ. xii. 17, 18.
*gap.
26ᵃ. xiii. 4ᵇ–6.
26ᵇ. xiii. 7–10, ending 'paciencia *nostra* et fides *nostra.*
*a gap, vv. 11–18 gone.
27ᵃ. xiv. 1.   quire 4.
27ᵇ. xiv. 2–5.
28ᵃ. xiv. 6, 7.
28ᵇ. xiv. 8.
29ᵃ. xiv. 9–12.
29ᵇ. xiv. 13.
30ᵃ. xiv. 14–16.
30ᵇ. xiv. 17–20.
31ᵃ. xv. 1.
31ᵇ. xv. 2–4.
*gap (xv. 5–xvi. 2).
32ᵃ. xvi. 3.
32ᵇ. xvi. 4–7.
33ᵃ. xvi. 8, 9.
33ᵇ. xvi. 10, 11.
34ᵃ. xvi. 12.
34ᵇ. xvi. 13–16.
35ᵃ. xvi. 17–21.

f. 35ᵇ. xvii. 1, 2.
36ᵃ. xvii. 3–5.
36ᵇ. xvii. 6–18.
37ᵃ. xxi. 1–8.
37ᵇ. xx. 11–15.
38ᵃ. xviii. 1–3.   4–20 omitted.
38ᵇ. xviii. 21–24.
39ᵃ. xix. 1–5.
39ᵇ. xix. 6–9ᵃ.
40ᵃ. xix. 9ᵇ, 10.
40ᵇ. xix. 11–16.
41ᵃ. xix. 17, 18.
41ᵇ. xix. 19.
42ᵃ. xix. 20, 21.
42ᵇ. xx. 1–3.
43ᵃ. xx. 4–6.
43ᵇ. xx. 7–9ᵃ.
44ᵃ. xx. 9ᵇ, 10.
*gap in the archetype.
44ᵇ. xxii. 6–15.
45ᵃ. xxii. 16–21.
The important *lacunae* are therefore :
1. vi. 1–4.
2. ix. 7–16.
3. x. 8–11, xi. 1, 2.
4. xiii. 1–4ᵃ (potestatem bestiae).
5. xiii. 11–18.
6. xv. 5–8, xvi. 1, 2.
7. xxi. 9–27, xxii. 1–5.
Portions of text purposely omitted are :
vii. 5–8.
xviii. 4–20.
Of the *lacunae* nos. 1–4 are caused by loss of leaves ; the others by defects in the archetype.

MEDIAEVAL SKETCH BOOK.
C.M.A. 6798, 79.   [1916.]

Vellum, 9⅘ × 7⅕, ff. 24 free, no text.   Cent. xiv late and xv early.
Lettered on the back : Monk's Draw : Book.

Collation : a⁴ (1 lines cover, 4 canc.) b⁴–f⁴ g² (2 lines cover).   The fourth leaf of f has been detached and sewn to the following one. In numbering I take account only of the free leaves.
That which lines the cover at the beginning is blank.
I will begin by enumerating the drawings on each leaf.

f. 1ᵃ. In pencil : A small figure of a knight in armour.   Part of another human figure.   A monster, four-legged, with human bust : faint.

Below, reversed: Sketch of a crucifix with the Virgin and St. John.

1[b]. Pattern for embroidery, in ink: Two almost complete rows of ornaments. Words in ink, smudged: W . . . wyt parfectysa.
In pencil : Several h's and possibly W M C.

2[a]. Ink (over pencil?): Nine grotesque monsters, for the most part quadrupeds with human heads, busts, or half-length bodies.

2[b], 3[a]. Outline and faint yellow-brown wash: One figure partly tinted with blue; one with black.

2[b]. Upper row from *l* : An angel facing *r*. Bearded figure with scroll facing *l*. Beardless man facing toward *l*. *r*., arm somewhat extended.
Lower row : Bearded figure facing *l*., holding book and pointing downward.
Bearded man, mantle over head; short drapery, ending just below the knee.
Two kings. The one on *l*. holds up what might be a vase.

3[a]. Upper row: Bishop seated, holding up both hands.
A woman looking towards him. In her *r*. hand she holds up what is perhaps a large cup, by the foot : on her *l*. a jug.
A woman with pendent sleeves looking in the same direction.
Lower row: Sketch of a pedestal. A woman with hands held up rather eagerly to *r*.
Two men facing *l*. ; very faint. One is beardless.

3[b]. Upper row: Bishop in chasuble and mitre, with book.
Monk, beardless, with book. Cowl thrown back.
Monk, beardless, with book. Cowl over head.
Lower row : Two youths in long robes facing *r*. The second has a book.
Maid holding a flower; a dog leaps up to her.
Pope facing *r*., in conical tiara, chasuble and pall.

4[a]. Upper row : Two seated maids. The first holds a chaplet ; the other has her arms oddly crossed.
A woman (devil in woman's form) facing *r*., with cap curled over at top.
A bearded man, almost nude, seated facing *l*. (a hermit?), a dagger at his waist.
Lower row : Three cardinals in broad hats without strings, all apparently beardless. Two have books.

4[b] (sqq.). Drawn across the breadth of the book : two figures on a page.
Two draped and bearded figures holding scrolls. (Apostles.)

5[a]. Two more in caps of the Jewish form without scrolls. (Prophets.)

5[b]. Two seated prophets with open books.

6[a]. A large half-length figure of the Virgin, in blue, with white veil and golden hair, holding a flower. The Child in her *r*. arm, with a pink drapery about the lower part of His body, stretches His arms to embrace her.
Above is *Santa Maria*.

6[b] has in upper part, a bearded, draped man seated on the ground looking up ; his hands in what may be called an "expository" attitude. A star (later) is rudely drawn in the *l*. upper corner.
Behind him, also seated, is a beardless figure holding forth an admonitory arm and raised finger.
The lower part of the page is blank.

7[a]. Two seated figures. Prophet partly coloured in blue, red, and purple : he wears a hat. St. Andrew holding a small cross fleury.

7[b]. Two prophets(?) in hats: the one on *r*. holds out a circular object (faintly drawn) by the rim.

8[a]. Three figures : A beardless man in long robes with pendent sleeves.
A bearded man in a hat, his mouth slightly open.
A youth in tunic and tight-fitting hose.

8^b. Three bareheaded men (apostles) with scrolls: one seated, two in animated attitudes.

9^a. Three apostles. One with a roll; the next, beardless, with a palm; the third, with a small cross, faintly drawn.

9^b. Animals in outline, probably inked over pencil drawing: names (xv) are written over some of them.

a chepe; an ewe suckling a lamb; a deer couchant.
A deer scratching his ear with his hind-leg. A beaver (?)
a horss. A donkey. *a talbott.*
Two rabbits, one disappearing into a burrow. *a catte.* A lion looking up. A hornless deer pursued by two hounds on a leash over which is written
a barce (?). A cat and a rat.
A dragon winged and two-legged, with knotted tail.
a coñe (rabbit) full face.

10^a sqq. Birds, etc., in colour.
A gryphon. A winged ox. Eagle flapping its wings. Eagle (?), small, with closed wings. Monkey in green jacket. Stag's head. Pelican in piety. Green parrot. Phoenix (blue), flames about its feet. A small bird with pinkish body and spread wings. A jay. A horned owl.

10^b. On this page are an eagle, three ducks, two red-legged partridges (*pertriche*), a goldfinch (*bolfynch*), *woodecoke*, and three other birds.

11^a. Heron (?), crane, *malard*, three more ducks, a swan (bluish), three cocks, a hen, three blue cranes, another bird.

11^b. Bat, squirrel, mermaid, hawks, a gull, a spoonbill, a cat, a nightjar, and other birds.

12^a. Hawks perched on gloves, hawk killing a drake, another drake, a *bwoll f(yn)ch*, another bird.

12^b. Woodpecker, partridge, duck.

13^a. Pair of pheasants, *pokocke* (peacock), tail feather with eye drawn separately, rook (?).

13^b. Peahen, and, in outline, a crane, called *heyryn*.

14^a sqq. Figures similar to those on f. 7 sqq.
Three seated figures. 1. Beardless, hooded, with scroll. 2. Beard, with raised hand. 3. Long-haired female (?) facing *r.* and with both hands out, as conversing.

14^b. Three figures. 1. Female pointing with *r.* hand at the ground: the *l.* on her knee. 2. Female, shaded in black, facing 1. 3. Black-shaded, in nunlike garb, striking a bell with a hammer.

15^a. Three seated apostles. 1. John, beardless, facing *r.* 2. Peter holding up keys. 3. Paul cross-legged with sword.

15^b. Two females, shaded in black, facing each other and conversing.
Christopher with staff bearing leaves at top. The Child with orb on his shoulder. Lightly coloured in white, purple, yellow, red, blue.

16^a. Coloured studies. 1. *l.* foreground: Man in pink tunic and blue hose, with *r.* arm raised in the attitude of a headsman. His victim not shown. 2. *l.*, St. George on foot in plate armour with white surcoat bearing red cross; beheading the dragon (two-winged and four-legged, with neck partly severed). A broken lance lies on *r.* The Princess kneels high up on *l.* 3. John Baptist in white seated on a rock caressing a nimbed Lamb on his arm.

16^b. Three studies of the nude, in outline inked over.

1. Eve with distaff. 2. Adam beardless. 3. Part of a nude male figure behind him.

17^a. (A strip is cut off the *r.* side of this leaf.) Rude pencil copy of the figure of Adam, and some rude heads.

E

17^b. Part of a design for a three-light window with cusping : drawn with dry-point.

18^a. Faint pencil sketch of a pomegranate pattern for embroidery. Small figure of an animal : bits of ornament. All in pencil.

18^b. Faint pencil sketch of a composition representing the Virgin crowned and nimbed : the Child (nude) on her arm turns away to *r.* and holds a flower ; tapestry is behind her. On *l.* kneels a nimbed beardless ecclesiastic holding a crosier.

19^a. Animals in colour, red and reddish-brown.

A lion (over it *lebarde*). A leopard.

An ox. A lion.

A gryphon. An ox.

A stag butting at a two-legged winged dragon on *r.*

19^b. Animals and grotesques in inked outline.

Hare, rabbits, squirrel, hedgehog, dogs, fox carrying off a pig pursued by a man with shovel, dragons or cockatrices, monkeys, cat, bears, camel, nude man riding a horse, another riding an elephant, fox and cock, man fighting lion, *a hoge* (hog) : twenty-nine in all.

20^a. Faint pencil sketch of a large figure of Christ in cope with large morse, holding the orb and blessing.

20^b. Section of a moulding boldly drawn.

21^a. Two sections of mouldings, and in pencil a figure of a beardless man in tunic and hat, with hair cut and curled, holding a flower and a sword.

21^b. Pencil sketches of heads, a monk, half-length of a man holding an apple or a ball in the palm of his hand, the Virgin and Child (small).

22^a. A large oblong piece cut out of the lower part of this leaf. In ink a monogram *ihc.* Capital M (Lombardic) crowned.

The Virgin crowned, seated, the (nude) Child embraces her : she holds a sceptre in her *l.* hand.

Part of a rather elaborate canopy pinnacled.

22^b. Three birds in pencil. A *talbotte*, in pencil. A dog running, in ink. A gryphon, in pencil. The word *gwodownlee* or *ga downlee*, in ink.

23^a. A very good head and part of figure of a king with curling hair and forked beard, rudely copied below.

23^b Blank.

24^a. A nude female figure, bending back, and with *r.* arm across her back, tinted with red. Small tree and rock on *r.*

Precii huius 3s. 4d., and a mutilated word a (or m) . . . tacŏns.

The main groups of subjects are :

a. The outline grotesques on 2^a 9^b 19^b.

b. The studies of draped figures on 2^b–4^a 6^b.

c. The larger studies on 4^b, 5, 7–9^a 14, 15.

d. The coloured studies of birds, etc. 10–13 19^a.

e. The coloured studies of figures 15^b 16^a.

f. The nude studies 16^b 24^a.

g. The architectural studies 17^b 20 21^a.

h. The embroidery patterns 1^b 18^a.

i. The pencil sketches 18^b 20^a.

k. The pen and ink drawings 22^a.

l. The Virgin and Child on 6^a.

not reckoning the smaller fragments of designs by various hands.

I should assign groups *b c* to one hand and *d e* to one hand, which can hardly be the same as for *b c*. *l*, which is the largest figure-drawing in the book, I do not think is by this artist, nor do I assign to him the nude studies.

This forms a most remarkable collection of studies by an English artist of the last years of the fourteenth century. They are, I think, intended for use both in paintings on a large scale (whether wall-paintings or easel-pictures) and also in illustrating books and in embroidery. For the latter purposes the studies of birds are specially appropriate. Bird-life seems to have been a favourite study of English artists. The vestments of the fourteenth century, worked in England, such as the cope of Pienza, the Syon cope, and others exemplify this; and so does the Sherborne Missal ornamented by Sifer Was, now at Alnwick Castle.[1] In this, many species of birds are figured with their names attached.

The studies of apostles, prophets, ecclesiastics, and saints are such as would be constantly needed by an artist engaged in the decoration of churches or the illuminating of books: the grotesques, as is well known, are most commonly to be found in the marginal decorations of manuscripts: with reference to others of the figure-studies, it has not hitherto been possible for me to determine their meaning; but most likely the interpretation of them will come in time.

VEGETIUS, ETC. IN FRENCH.
C.M.A. 6760. 41, 6761. 42, 6796. 77. [1938².]

Vellum, $9\frac{7}{10} \times 6\frac{1}{5}$, ff. 103, 30 lines to a page. Cent. xiv. Second half well written: in brown ink.

Bound with Caxton's Boke of the fayt of arms and of Chyualrye of Christine de Pisan. 2 fo. peuples.

Collation: 1^8–10^8 (wants 6–8) 11^2 12^8–14^8.

1. The description of the contents of this MS. given by M. Paul Meyer in *Romania*, xxv. 414-19 needs hardly any addition save some notice of the pictures.

Cambridge, Magdalene Coll. (collection S. Pepys, no. 1938). Ce ms. est relié avec un exemplaire des *Faythes of armes of chyvalrye*, ouvrage imprimé par Caxton et traduit, comme on sait, de Christine de Pisan. C'est un livre d'une exécution soignée, écrit en lettre de forme dans la seconde moitié du xive siècle. L'ornementation est assez riche. Il n'y a pas de doute qu'il a dû être fait pour quelque grand personnage. Dans la miniature de présentation on voit un héraut d'armes agenouillé présenter

---

[1] Recently partly reproduced for the Roxburghe Club by the Duke of Northumberland, under the editorship of Mr. J. A. Herbert.

un livre à un roi d'Angleterre (?) assis sur un fauteuil à dais. Le héraut d'armes porte les armes parties de France et d'Angleterre (les trois lions d'or sur champ de gueules). Au bas de la page se trouvent des armes qu'un plus habile saura sans doute identifier. Ce sont des armes parties. À senestre, un écartelé que je suppose avoir été de France et d'Angleterre : le champ de gueules et les trois lions d'or (2 et 3) ne sont pas douteux, mais les deux autres quartiers (1 et 4) sont bien effacés. A dextre, une ancre d'or sur champ d'azur.

Premiers mots du second feuillet : *peuples qui leur sont.* L'ouvrage commence ainsi (il n'y a pas de pagination) :

Le premier livre

Ci commence le livre et l'istoire de Flave Vegece, des fais et proesses de chevalerie, translaté de latin en françois, qui parle en brief des fais des Rommains.

(Ici la miniature de présentation.)

Ci apres s'ensuit le prologue du livre. Cap. .j.

Ci comence le livre de Vegece, de chevalerie, translaté de latin en françois par maistre Jehan de Vignay, de l'ordre de Hault pas, lequel livre contient .iiij. livres complez.

Le premier livre monstre et enseigne de l'ancien temps, qui dit ainsi que a nul n'affert mieux a savoir plusseurs choses que aux princes, pour raison de gouverner le (*sic*) province a leur honneur et au proufit de leur peuple.

Le secont livre monstre comment le souvrain d'une bataille doit deviser et amenistrer toutes les choses qu'il convient a host vivre et a son cors garder.

Le tiers livre si devise queulx engins et queulx mangonneaux et que pierres on doit avoir, et quelx armes.

Le quart si parle de fortes batailles de terre et de eaue et de manieres des tours qui y sont.

S'ensuyt le prologue du translateur.

Tout ausi comme dit Segons li philosophes, letre si est garde de ystoire. Et pour ce fut coustume aux anciens qu'i mistrent leur cure et leur entente a cognoistre les vertus et les natures des chosses, de commettre en la lettre la science et les sens qu'il avoient acquis par grant treval et par leur exerciter, pour ce qu'il peüst profiter a leurs successeurs, car memoire est escoulourjable ou oubliable et tost perist. . . . . .

Début de la traduction :

Cy apres s'ensuit le prologue de l'aucteur qui ce livre composa de atin en françois par le comandement de l'empereeur rommain qui vivoit en ce temps, et s'ensuit comment il offry son livre a l'empereeur.

En l'ancien temps furent acoustumées les estudes dez bones ars metre en lettre, et ce qui est ramené quant ou livre offrir aux princes, si est car nule riens n'est a droit commencie, se après Dieu ne l'otroie, qui est li souvrain emperiere, ne a nul n'affiert mieux savoir pluseurs choses ne meilleurs que au prince, lequel sens et doctrine si puist proufiter a touz ses subgiès. . . . . .

L'ouvrage se termine ainsi :

Je cuide que dezoremaiz est il temps de soy retraire de la descipline d'armes, car en telz choses le souvrain usage treuve souvent plus d'art que l'ancienne doctrine ne demonstre.

Explicit totum. Deo gracias.
Ci finist Vegece, de la chose de chevalerie. Deo gracias.

Ci fenist le livre Flave Vegece, de la chose qui dist est en chevalerie, translaté de latin en françois, mot a mot, selonc le latin ; et contient .iiij. livres, desquieulx, ou premier, il y a .xxviij. chapistres, ou secont .xxv., ou tiers .xxix. et ou quart .xlvij.[1]. Ce sont en somme par tout le livre .vj^{xx}. et .viij. chappistres.

Explicit. Deo gracias.

Le manuscrit contient encore divers opuscules ; à savoir :

1. — *Le Dit des trois morts et des trois vifs*. Rédaction publiée par M. de Montaiglon, dans son édition française de l'*Alphabet de la mort*, par Hans Holbein (1856), d'après le ms. B. N. fr. 378, le seul où ce dit eût été reconnu jusqu'alors. Depuis j'en ai trouvé, au Musée britannique, deux autres copies, l'une complète, l'autre abrégée ; voir le *Bulletin de la Société des anciens textes*, année 1881, pp. 46 et 71. Une quatrième fait partie du ms. B. N. fr. 957, fol. 132, et une cinquième occupe les derniers feuillets du psautier de Bonne de Luxembourg, femme du roi Jean (*Catalogue Didot*, vente de 1882, p. 6). Avec le ms. de Magdalene Coll. nous arrivons à six, et assurément il existe d'autres exemplaires de la même composition. Notons que dans le ms. 957, comme dans celui que nous étudions en ce moment, le dit est précédé d'un prologue que n'ont pas les autres manuscrits [2] et qui était destiné à expliquer une peinture placée en tête de la poésie. Cette sorte d'introduction est ici écrite à lignes pleines, comme de la prose, ainsi du reste que le commencement du dit. Les vers sont assez souvent incorrects, comme aussi dans le ms. 957. Je respecte la disposition du ms., marquant par des traits verticaux la fin de chaque vers :

Ci commence l'istoire de trois mors et de trois vifs.[3]
Ceste diverse portraiture | Nous presente une aventure | Qu'il avint a la voille [4] Saine. | Trois jouvenceaus en une plaine, | Si come jounesse [5] leur cuer maine, | S'esbatoient en la verdure | Maiz tost mua leur joie en paine, | Car aventure leur [a]maine | Trois corps d'orrible figure. | Mais espontable outre mesure. | Moult estoient cilz trois joynes hommes | Lieux [6] et jovans et drus | Ains qu'eüssent lez mors veüz, | Car d'avoir avoient grant somme. | Il n'avoit entre Saine et Romme | en leur temps plus riche d'eulx, | Mais moult fut leur sanc esmeüz | Quant il orent les morz veüz, | Laiz et hydeux, plus noirs que gomme, | Qu'il n'est nul qui sache la somme.

---

[1] Corr. *.xlvj.*, leçon du ms. de Paris.

[2] Il est à remarquer que le ms. 957 offre à d'autres égards des points de contact avec le ms. Pepys : il renferme les articles 2 à 7 indiqués ci-après.

[3] A la suite de cette rubrique se trouve une miniature : à gauche, les trois vifs à cheval ; à droite, les trois morts, et, entre ces deux groupes, une croix monumentale.

[4] Ms. 957 *vielle*.

[5] *Sic* ms. 957, corr. *com*, ou *jouvens*.

[6] Corr. *liez*, d'après le ms. 957.

Coment le premier vif parle a son compaingnon.
Le premier vif dit :
Compains vois tu ce que je voie? | A paine que je ne me desvoie; | De grant paour le cuer me tremble. | Vois ces .iij. mors laiz et hydeux | Et horribles divers,[1] | Toux porris et mangiés de vers.

Le dit se termine ainsi, avec le discours du troisième mort :

De vostre vanité retraire.
Si gardez que vous n'aiez honte.
Laissiez le mal pour le bien faire,
Si qu'a Jhesu Crist puisse plaire
Quant ce vendra au jour de compte.
Ci fenist de .iij. mors. et .iij. vifs. Amen.

2. — Un poème en 22 quatrains, sur la parabole du mauvais riche, dont on connaissait déjà une copie dans le ms. B. N. fr. 957, fol. 118; voy. P. Paris, *Mss. français*, VII, 339. Début :

Devant l'uys au riche homme le ladre trespassa;[2]
Pour la [grant] faim qu'il ot forment se dementa.
Quant le ladre longuement devant la porte esta
Le riche homme[3] n'en tint conte qui moult bien l'escouta.

Le ladre au riche homme fist un courtois reclain :
"En l'onneur de Dieu qui est le roy souvrain,[4]
"Donne moy, se te plaist, un peu de menu pain;
"Avis m'est que le cuer me part, tant ay grant faim. . . ."

3. — Suivent dix quatrains moraux qui se trouvent aussi dans le ms. 957, fol. 119 v°. Début :

Ci apres s'ensuit de la faussete du monde.
Le monde sez amis par raison deshonneure,[5]
Maiz, quant ilz cuident estre seür et a desseure,
Adonc leur faut le corps et la mort leur cuert seure :
Seingnorie et hautesse perdent en petit d'eure.
Moult est folz qui s'amour en ce monde emploie . . .

4. — *Le despit du corps*, dont on connaissait déjà une quinzaine de manuscrits, et qui a été imprimé dans Bartsch et Horning, *La langue et la littérature françaises*, col. 547 et suiv., d'après un manuscrit seulement. Cf. *Hist. litt.*, XXIII, 283. Début :

Ci apres s'ensuit du despit du cors.
Corps, en toy n'a point de savoir,
Car tu convoites trop avoir,
Deniers. richesses et vair et gris. . . .

5. — Débat du corps et de l'âme (*Visio Philiberti*), poème en quatrains,

---

[1] Le ms. 957 a une leçon différente, mais corrompue; il faut lire :
Vois tu la ces .iij. mors enssamble
Cum il sunt hideus et divers.
[2] Ms. 957 *s'aresta.*   [3] Corr. *hom.*
[4] Ms. 957 *qui est roy souverain.*   [5] Ms. 957 *par trayson honneure.*

dont je connais une vingtaine de mss., et maintes fois imprimé, depuis 1485, avec la *Danse Macabre*.[1] Début :

> *Ci apres s'ensuit l'altercation ou la desputoison qui est faite entre le corps et l'ame.*
>> Une grant vision en ce livre est escrite
>> Jadis fu revelée a dam Philbert l'ermite....

6 — *Je vais mourir*, pièce en sixains, où chaque couplet commence et finit par *Je vois morir*. C'est encore une pièce qui a été bien souvent copiée. Elle a été publiée d'après le ms. B. N. fr. 1555, où elle a pour titre *le Mireuer du monde*, par Méon, à la suite des *Vers sur la mort*, p. 73 et suiv. (Paris, Crapelet, 1835). Début :

> *Ci apres commence un tres bon enseignement pour un chascun de quelque estat qu'il soit homme ou femme.*
>> Je vois morir, venés avant.
>> Tuit cil qui ores estes vivant
>> Joynes et viel et foible et fort
>> Nous sommes tous jugiés a mort 's.

7. — *Le Doctrinal aux simples gens*, de Gui de Roie. On en possède de nombreux mss., par ex. B. N. fr. 957, 1865, 1879, 1880. Cet opuscule a été souvent imprimé ; voir Brunet, *Manuel*, ROYE (GUI DE). Début :

> *Ci commence le Doctrinal dez simples gens, qui enseingne plusseurs biens ou nom de Jhesu Crist.*
>> Ou nom de Jhesu Crist, c'est ici une bonne doctrine pour briefment et pleinement enseignier les simples gens a bien vivre et a bien confesser. Et est compillé de tout ce qui s'ensuit.

The pictures in the volume are of fair quality : the first has been somewhat damaged.

1. f. 1. Ground red, with pattern of yellow lines framing squares. On *l.*, a bearded emperor throned under green and gold canopy. He wears a robe party per pale of *az.*, semée of fleurs-de-lis *or*, and *or* an eagle *sable* (only partly seen) : he holds up a sword : an attendant by him. The man who kneels on *r.* presenting a book is in plate armour with surcoat bearing the following arms : Party per pale dexter quarterly of England and France ancient : sinister *azure*, a cross ancre *or* between 4 martlets of the second. The same arms are in the lower border, but in the dexter part the French quarterings are erased.

2. Lib. II, f. 17[b]. Ground with pattern of gold lines on pink and lozenges of black and white vertically divided. A king with grey beard in armour, and surcoat *az.*, three crowns *or*, attended by two men in scarlet and green, receives a book from a kneeling man habited as in no. 1. Here (as in no. 1) his surcoat bears a label of four points *arg.*, a lion rampant *gules* on each.

3. Lib. III, f. 32[b]. King nimbed (?) on *r.* with two attendants. Surcoat *azure*, semée of fleurs-de-lis *or*. To him kneel a queen with the same bearings on her robe, and a youth with surcoat of six parts (?) France and ? England. They present a book to the king, who may be meant for St. Louis.

---

[1] Voy. Brunet, *Manuel*, II, 490 ; E. Picot, *Catal. de la Bibl. James de Rothschild*, I, 354.

Lib. IV has no picture.

4. *Dit des trois mors*, etc. f. 78. Ground with similar pattern. In *c.*, a white cross on a base. On *l.*, the three youths on horses, in consternation : one has a hawk. On *r.* the three corpses. Those on *r.* and *l.* are nude, that on *l.* carries a coffin lid : the second is in a shroud.

5. *Histoire du mauuais riche homme.* f. 80. Scarlet ground hatched with gold lines. On *l.*, Dives and his wife, in blue, at table : an attendant turns to Lazarus, who sits on *r.* holding a white object with three petals—probably a rattle. Two dogs at his feet.

6. *Laltercacion entre le corps et lame.* f. 85ᵇ. Green ground with pattern of gold line. A bearded man in bed covered with red ; head to *l.* Above it in air a devil with a book. On the foot of the bed stands a small nude figure, the soul.

The last tract ends imperfectly

La bouche pour ly mercier (catchword : et loer).

There are some scribbles of Elizabeth's time on margins, but they do not seem to throw light on the ownership of the book except one on f. 23 :

Willm̄ gorges hand the yovnge(r)

and one on 95ᵇ (xvi) Robert fframblyn of Northelmham in the county of Norfolk.

A notarial mark is on the same page.

SIR JOHN MANDEVILLE.

C.M.A. vac.   [1955.]

Vellum and paper, 10 × 7⅘, ff. 76, 30 lines to a page. Cent. xv. In an ugly current hand. Binding of the usual Pepysian style.

Collation : 1¹²–6 ¹² 7⁴. Outer and middle sheets of vellum in each quire, except the last, where only the outer sheet is of vellum : the rest paper, f. 1ᵃ blank.

Text.   1ᵇ·

For as moche as þe lond ouyr þe see ⸳ þat ys to say þe holylonde that men calle þe londe of byheste

There are marginalia in ink and pencil of cent. xvi–xvii.

The last paragraphs are :

There be many oþer contres and meruayles, etc. ...

And y Johñ Maundewyle kny3t þou3e y were vnworþy. ...

So þat he wᵗ hys auyse & consayle dude examyne þys boke. ...

And I pray to alle þo that rede yn þys boke ...

—he þᵗ ys yn trynyte ffadyr & sone & holy goste þat lyueth & regneth wyth oute ende. Amen.

Maundeuyle.

In a sixteenth-century hand : Mandeville's reputed epitaph.   76ᵃ

In the Church of the Gulielmites Cloyster without yᵉ walle of leige with this inscription

hic jacet vir nobilis D. Jo. de Mandeville, etc.

a. d. Mᵒ cccᵒ lxxiᵒ mensis Nouembris die xvijᵒ.

76ᵇ covered with paper.

TRACTS IN ITALIAN.

C.M.A. vac. [1998.]

Paper, 10⅗ × 7½, pp. 296, 26 lines to a page.   Cent. xviii (just after 1700).   Well written.

Title-page :
Brevi Caratteri di 22 Cardinali de' piu eminenti é papabili insieme con Diversi altri Trattati manuscritti spettanti principalmente alle Pratiche della Corte Romana

Raccolti in Roma nel anno Santo 1700.

A full table of Contents follows.

12. Instruttione data all' Ill.ᵐ. . . . Signore Marchese N. N. Ambasciator di Spagna.   261

13. Relazione dell'arrivo delle Falere di Francia à Baia, e regali mandati al General Novaglier come anco il pranso fatto in Napoli al detto Generale et officiali Francesi dal vice Rè Duca Medina Coeli Li 2 Settembre 1698.   277

14. Nota del Regale fatto dall' Em. S. Card. Carlo Barbarino alla Maestà della Regina Vedoua di Polonia Maria Casimira Sabato li 28 Marzo 1699.

15. Rinfresco ò Regale fatto dalla Sᵗᵃ di N. S. Innoc. XII (alla medesima) 25 Mar. 1699 a hore 22.   284

16. Ristretto della Congregatione tenuta sopra l'esame dell' Editto contra l'immodestia del uestire delle donne.   285

17. Metodo dell' Academia Ecclesiastica promessa da Monsig. Illᵐᵒ e Revᵐᵒ Gio Rasponi dignissimo Vescovo della Città di Forli. Da farsi nel di lui Palazzo Vescovale Lanno 1700.   293

Ending: In Forli nella Stamperià Episcopale 1700 Con Licenza Superiorum.

G. WITHER.

C.M.A. vac.   [1999.]

Paper, 10⅗ × 6⁷⁄₁₀, ff. 47, 40 lines to a page. Cent. xvii, after 1625. Well written.

The History of the Pestilence or The proceedinge of Justice & Mercy Manifested Att the great Assize holden about London, in the yeere 1625. wherein soe many were executed by that Plague.

Recorded ffaithfully wᵗʰ many pertynent Circumstances for the future benefite of all theis Kingdoms, and dedicated vnfainedly to the Glorie of Almightie God.

By George Wither: whoe being present at that Arraignment (and deserving death) was acquited by the free pardon of Mercy.

Oh come hether and hearken, etc,: Ps. 66. 14 (followed by Ps. 91. 6, and Ps. 51. 15).

On f. 2. The dedication in prose to the King.

The first Canto begins with a proem in octosyllables:
> Our Aucthor first wᵗʰ God begins,
> Describes his Anger for our Synns, etc.

The poem itself is in decasyllabic couplets, beginning:
> The Storme is past, and loe, wee now obteyne
> The cheerefull brightnes of Gods face againe.

Canto II begins f. 23 and ends f. 46ᵇ.

I the faults of both
Have shewed soe that neither I abuse ;
Now, those that like it, may : the rest may chuse
The end of the
Second Canto.

This MS. is mentioned in *D. N. B.* as being in the author's autograph, and unpublished. It is, however, a draft or version of the first two Cantos of Wither's *Britain's Remembrancer*, published 1628.

MEDULLA GRAMMATICES.

C. M. A. 6794. 75.   [2002¹.]

Paper, 10¾ × 7⅘, ff. 136, double columns of 40 lines. Cent. xv late. In two hands, the first of which is the better : the second begins at f. 49.

Bound with a copy of the Dyalogus Creaturarum printed by Gerard Leeuw, Gouda 1481.

Collation : 1¹²–4¹² | 5⁸–16⁸.

Late title :

An excellent diccionary, none better in prent : for the number of wordes contayned.

Prol. Hec est Regula generalis pro toto libro
—fructuum gramatice pueris do sub breuitate
hic liber intitulatur Medulla gramatice
Almus a um an*gli*ce meke
Aron est quidam Mons [a mountayne xvi]
A preposicio an*gli*ce ffor
· etc.

Ends 136ᵇ : zoticus a um .i. vitalis
zozimus a um .i. viuax vel humidus
Et cetera.

A note beginning Inter vocales, and ending
Resarcio . cis et prosesar ut predicatur in versibus
Expl. medulla gramatice.
Explicit iste liber scriptor sit crimine liber
Huius scriptoris requiescat in omnibus horis
Spiritus in Christo dum mundo transit ab isto.   Amen.
Orate pro scriptore.

An account of the Medulla Gramatice is given by Albert Way in *Prompt. Parvulorum*, Camd. Soc. 1865, ii, p. 6, with a list of the MSS. (including this one). Harl. 2270 begins and ends in the same way as this. A later title ascribes it to ' Galfridus.'

CHAUCERIAN PIECES.
C.M.A. 6786. 67.   [2006.]

Paper, 10⅜ × 7, ff. 196, single and double columns, in various hands, generally good but current, of cent. xv.

Collation: 1 (eight) 2¹⁴ : for the rest I find it impracticable.

Middles of gatherings occur after pp. 68, 86, 98, 110, 130, 146, 166, 180, 196, 218 | 232, 244, 256, 276, 288, 304, 316, 328, 340, 358, 372 | 382.

Catchword, p. 112.

Gaps after ff. 114, 224, 380, 384.

I. 38-9 lines to a page.

1. The complaynt of yᵉ blak knyght (? in Stow's hand). By Lydgate.   p. 1

Skeat, *Chaucer*, vii, p. 245. This copy was consulted by him. It was written by a northern scribe.

2. Temple of glas. Title in the same hand. By Lydgate.   17

Change of hand at p. 45 : 42 lines to a page. This hand seems to continue (with very slight interruptions) to p. 224 inclusive.

This copy is described by Schick, *Temple of Glas*, E.E.T.S., p. xx. The first part, pp. 17-44, was written by a northern scribe.

3. Legend of good women. Title in the same hand.   53

viz. Prologue.

Cleopatre, p. 67.

Thisbe, beginning at l. 72 (777). Come Pyramus, 71.

pp. 71, 72 being in another hand.

Dido, 75.

Isophele and Medea, 88. ll. 1–10 only. On the text see Skeat III. xlix, whose symbol for it is P.

Continuing on the same page with

4. Pryer a n͞re dame per Chaucer. Skeat, i. 261. This copy is not used by him. Carleton Brown, no. 152.   [88

Almyghty and almerciable quene.

Chaucer's ABC.

Ending with the fourth line of stanza H. Of mercy put that in his remembraunce.

The rest of p. 90 is blank.

5. The booke of ffame (xvi). Skeat, I. xiii.   91

pp. 92–114 are in double column.

Ends in Bk. III (l. 1843, Skeat).

Madam quod he soth to tell
I am that ilk shrew wys.

6. Complaint of Mars and Venus. Skeat, i. 323. This copy not used. 115

The title, almost cut off, seems to have been *The boocke of Thebes* (as in Harl. 7333): so Miss Hammond suggests, and I agree.

The Compleynt of Mars (alone). 119

The Compleynt of Venus (alone). Skeat, i. 400. This copy is used as ms. P. 122

7. Pleyntyf encountre fortune. (Fortune, Skeat, i. 383.) 124

8. The parlament of fowles. Skeat, i. 335. 127

Ending with l. 667 To euery fowle nature yaf his make.

Caret follows in the sixteenth-century hand.

9. History of the Three Kings. (English version of John of Hildesheim. Printed by Horstmann, E.E.T.S.) 143

Syth of these thre worschypfull kynges

Ending p. 183: worshipd of alle maner of nacōns in to this day and so thus endeth þe translacōn of these .iij. wurschipfull kynges, etc.

Expl. vite et Translacionum Trium regum.

10. Letter of Prester John. 183

Prestes Jhon that is lorde of Jnde & alle the kyngdomes & kynges þat bene vndere hym. They vse on the xii day that whe clep the fest of the Epiphanie

Ending p. 189, on the "secte þᵗ ben cleped mandopolos."

—to the wheche blisse he bryng vs alle þᵗ in heuene above alle kynges & seintes sitten & regnen Crist Jhesus bryng vs alle. Amen.

p. 190 (pasted over) has some scribbles which are not important.

11. The Serpent of Division by Lydgate (War of Caesar and Pompey). 191

Whilom as olde bokes maken mencion wherin the noble famouse Cite of Rome

Of my lytill konnyng to put in remembraunce, etc. qᵈ J. de C.

Lenvoie. This litill prose declareth in figure 209

. . . . . .

Of Pompeie and Cesar Julius.

p. 210, pasted over, has some ill-written lines.

12. Inc. Cato ("Parvus Cato," by Benedict Burgh, ed. Förster, *Engl. Stud.* 36. 4. Carleton Brown, no. 2533). 211

Prol. When I aduertyse my remembraunce

And see how fele erren grevowsly.

Six-line stanzas. The corresponding Latin (Cum animaduerterem) written on the *r.*

Lenvoy. 8 lines. Behold my maister this litill tretyse   212

doth as he seith wyth alle your hole entente. Expl.
Text. Si deus est animus, etc.   213
   ffor why that god is in warldy thy wytte
   Of man and geveth hym vnderstandyng.
Pars prima ends p. 223. Of Pars secunda only the prologue and a few
lines remain. Ending p. 224.
   Than rede Chacer in his old ditee
   Wheche tellyth alle men in her propre qualite.

II. A large upright hand.   31 lines to a page.
13. Here begynneth Chaucers tale of Melibee.   225
   A yongman called Melibeus
   —— blisse þat neuer hath ende.
Here endeth Chauceres owne tale of Thopas and of Melibee and
Prudence his wyfe.
Here begynneth the Prologe of the Persones Tale.   276
The tale begins p. 279.
There is a marked change of hand on p. 346 to one of a legal type,
which, though it becomes a good deal rougher, seems to continue to
p. 377 inclusive.
   On p. 377 is Chaucer's Retractation.
   Two leaves are stuck together after p. 377. The second has on it
Johēs Kiriet or Kiriel in a large hand.

III. A largish hand.   28 lines to a page mostly. Earlier, I think, than
the last.
14. The Complaint of Mars.   Without title.   378
   ll. 1–28, 57–84, 29–56.
   The Complaint of Venus, ll. 45–82 (end).   381
15. "The Compleint of Anelida quene of Hermenye vpon false
Arcite of Thebes."   382
   ll. 1–311, omitting one stanza (290–8).
   Ending imperfectly.
   Skeat, i. 373–6.
16. The last two lines of *Fortune* (no. 7).   385
17. Lenuoie de Chaucer a Scogan.   Skeat, i. 396.   385
18. Prier a nr̄e Dame *per* Chaucer.   386
   A second copy of no. 4, leaving off with the same line, which does not
finish the page.
19. La compleint de Chaucer a sa Bourse voide.   Skeat, i. 405.   388
20. Le boñ Counsell de Chaucer (Truth, Skeat, i. 390).   389

ll. 1–21, omitting the Envoy.

21. Merciles Beaute. Skeat, i. 387. There is no title in the MS. 390
Skeat's text is from this copy.

The text ends on p. 391. *Explicit* in red.

Below is written :

Iste liber constat Willelmo ffetypace mercerii london.

Iste liber constat Thome W.

p. 392 is pasted over but has nothing on it.

There follows, very carefully written by a copyist employed by Pepys :
A collation of these MSS. Fragments of Chaucer, no. 1074 B, wth his
Printed Works, no. 1281.

This collation marks the principal defects of the MS. as compared
with the printed edition. It occupies four pages.

As to the distribution of hands, Miss E. P. Hammond, in *Mod. Lang.
Notes*, 1904, p. 196, distinguishes six, viz. :

A   pp. 1–44.
B   45–142.
C   143–224.
D   225–346 sub fine ⎫ These seem to me the latest hands in
E   346–377   ⎬   the volume.
F   378–end.   ⎭

I incline to think that hands B and C may be the same.

Other accounts of the MS. are in Todd's *Illustrations*, p. 116;
Chaucer Soc., *Supplementary Parallel Texts*.

SCOTCH SURVEY OF THE PRAYER-BOOK.

C.M.A. vac.   [2007.]

Paper, 10⅘×7³⁄₁₀, ff. 27, 32 lines to a page. Cent. xvii. Fairly
written.

Boards covered with purple paper patterned in gold. Title written on
an engraved frame cut out and pasted on the side.

The Scotch Survey of the English Service-Book. 1638. MSS.

1. In the survey of the errors of the service book theise 38 seuerall
particulers are expressed, viz.   1

1. Dangers in alteracons.

.   .   .   .   .

38. Of the number of sacraments.

A Brief Survey of the Errors of the service booke now imposed vpon vs
the Nobilitie Ministrie gentrie and the whole Comunalitie of Scotland. 2

1. Of Dangers in alteracons.

All changes & alteracons though but in policie and albeit to may tend even to the better yett they are very dangerous, etc.

End f. 19ᵃ: particulerly necessary to some though not necessary to all. ffinis.

19ᵇ. blank.

2. A particuler Answere by a private Minister Concerning the Kneeling at receaving the Sacrament.

   1. It is agreable to the example of Christ & the Apostles all times for the common forme of sitting, etc.   20
      Containing 20 Articles.

   3. A Coppie of a letter sent from the Churches of Germanie vnto the Churche of Scotland.   Aᵒ. 1638.   22
      Wonderfull are all the works of the Almightie God
      —done unto all such as persever unto the end.

   4. A letter from the bodie of the kingdome of Scotland vnto their appointed Commissioners.   23ᵇ
      Right honorable & potent Earle . . . Wee Sions heartie wellwishers to the last dropp of our blood
      —Quitt ye like men & be strong.

   5. The Duke of Lennox speech to his Maᵗⁱᵉ concerning the Proposition of warr for Scotland.   25
      Most graceous Soueraigne

I am not altogether insensible of this bussines—
—but neither knowe where to beginne it nor greatly care where or when to end it.

LYDGATE.
                C.M.A. 6790. 71.   [2011.]
Vellum, 10⁷⁄₁₀ × 7½, ff. 2+80, 32 lines to a page.   Cent. xv.   In a very clear, rather tall, and slightly sloping hand.

Collation: *a*² 1⁸–10⁸.

On the fly-leaves is a table of contents in a hand of cent. xv early going as far as f. 45.

   1. Lydgate's Destruction of Thebes.
   Prol.: Whan phebus passed was the Rame
          Midde of Aprill and in to þe boll came.
   Good decorative initial and partial border.
   The prologue ends f. 3ᵇ, and than begynnyth þe tale.
             Sirs quod I sith of youre curtesy
             I entred am in to youre company.

Secunda pars, f. 18.

Tercia pars, f. 41.

Ends 76^b: And Joy eternall whan we hense wende
        And of my tale thus y make an ende. Amen.

Here endeth the distruccioun of Thebes.

Secundum lidgate Monke off Bury.

2. A lenvoye to alle prynces that be disposed to be lecherous   77
    O noble prynces off hige discressioun

  .   .   .   .

    Anoynt youre Eres, to make you lecherous.
        Expl. desolacioun of Rome.

3. This is the letter that daun John lidgate Monke of Bury sent to
Humphreyduke of Gloucester for mony for making of Bochas.   78
    Right myghty prynse and hit be youre wille
    Condiscende leyser for to take
    To see þe content of this litill Bylle.

  .   .   .   .

    God sende sone a gladder letuary
    With a clere sone of plate & of coignage.
        Expl. litera de dan John lidgate.

On 79^b (xvi). Wyne, wemen, & tonges inconstant
        Mayke of y^e Sapient an ynanorante.

On 80^a. Edwardus sextus dei gratia, etc.

80^b pasted over, blank.

CHRONICLE OF MARTINUS POLONUS, ETC., IN ENGLISH.

C.M.A. 6719. 4, 6720. 5, 6756. 37.   [2014.]

Vellum, $10\frac{7}{10} \times 7\frac{1}{5}$, ff. 61, double columns of 60 lines. Cents. xiv–xv. In
a very beautiful clear small hand: black ink. Initials in blue with some
red flourishing.

Collation: 1^8 2^8 $3^6/4^8$ 5^3 (wants 6–8)/6^8–8^8 (7 canc.) 9 (three).

It belonged to Charles Fairfax 1619. Ex dono Humfredi Chambers
de Lincolns Inne Armig. senescal. deput. Westm.

He has written a note of the contents on the fly-leaf.

1. A version of the Chronicle of Martinus Polonus.

Ihesu cryst was Ibore in þe two and fourty ʒeer of Octauyan.

The headline for alternate pages is *Emperours* and *Popes*, but in the
text they are not kept to alternate pages, as is commonly the case in the

Latin copies.   The last Emperor is Frederick II.   A paragraph follows:
After ffederykes deþ þe Emperoures cesseden at Rome, etc.
... Conradus ffederykes sonne after ffederykes deeþ, etc.
—And his leches ȝeuen him a medecyne to haue heled him & hit
enpoysoned him.
The last Pope is John XXI, ending:
    ȝit he lyffed fro þe Saturday tyl it was Sonday nyȝt after.   20ᵃ
The remainder of 20ᵇ and 21, 22, are ruled and have headlines, but
are blank.

2. At the bottom of 22ᵇ is this note: Euangelium Nicodemi vides alio
libro MS. antiquo meo qui nuper Prioratui de Parco Ludae (Louth Park)
spectabat et sermone Latino.   Probably in Fairfax's hand.
Title (in the same hand, I think):
    Nichodemus his Gospell (ut Seldenus asserit)   23

It is the poem Titus and Vespasian or the Destruction of Jerusalem
printed from this MS. by Rudolph Fricker, *Archiv f. neu. Spr.* cxi.
285 sqq. and cxii. 25 sqq. (1903–4) with a description of the MS. under
the title *Vindicta Saluatoris*.   Edited from other MSS. by J. A. Herbert,
Roxburghe Club, 1905.
Inc.   Goddes men vnderstondeþ nowe   (ed. Herbert, l. 815)
            And I schal ȝou telle howe
            The ȝewes dude Ihesu to dede
            Thoruȝ feble counseil & false rede.
This copy is imperfect, lacking somewhat over 800 lines at the
beginning.   Carleton Brown no. 1171.

It ends 35ᵇ.   Iosephus þan byhelde þis man
            And comforte him þo he bygan
            And þe styward dude also
            Wiþ fayre semblañte & speche þerto.   (l. c., l. 4010)
Herbert's text runs to 5184 lines.

3. Fragments of the Chronicle of Robert of Gloucester, viz.:
ll. 4216–5811 (ed. W. A. Wright, Rolls Series).
            But ȝif þei se nede.
            —As in þe ȝere of grace: sixty and fyftene.   51ᵇ

Here follow ll. 1–18 (and catchword half of line 19) of Appendix II
(l. c., ii. p. 833).
            And fulle fyftene ȝeer   57ᵇ
                        —to lyen in a stoon
            But he myȝt noȝt.

Then ll. 8557–9137.   52

    Wyllyames douȝter

         —þer was no dowte ne fere.

Followed by Appendix XX (l. c., ii. 838):

    Tho come Steuen þe Bloys

    —He wanne þe signorye: were þei neuer so prout.   62^b

The MS. is ε in Wright's edition: see I. xlv.

THE SEVEN PSALMS. PETER IDLE, ETC.

C.M.A. 6788. 69.   [2030.]

Paper, $10\frac{3}{4} \times 7\frac{9}{10}$, ff. 184, 32 lines to a full page, but for the most part 28. Cent. xvi. In a clear, but not beautiful hand.

Boards covered with purple paper patterned in gold.

The collation is not practicable.

On f. 1. This Book was Henery yᵉ 6 King of England. The Author was Bourn in Kent as he saith him selfe in thes folloing worck.

John Bagford 1682. Bagford's name occurs elsewhere in the book.

Contents.

1. The Penitential Psalms in English verse, by Th. Brampton: seven-line stanzas: a verse of the Latin Psalm prefixed to each, and the burden Ne reminiscaris domine affixed throughout. Carleton Brown, no. 964, ed. W. H. Black, Percy Society, vii.   1

Begins imperfectly (stanza 7, l. 7).

    My synfull werkys bothe more & lesse

    Ne reminiscaris domine.

Miserere mei domine quoniam infirmus sum sana me domine, etc.

                          (Ps. vi. 3.)

    Sethyn thou woldest no man were I loste,

    have mercy on me for I am syke.

A leaf lost in Ps. l (li) after f. 7

Ends imperfectly:

    Notam fac michi viam in qua ambulem, etc. (Ps. cxlii. 8).

        Teche me lord the redi way

        That I may my soule save

    .   .   .   .   .   .

        And devoutely cry & crave

        Ne reminiscaris domine.

Stanzas 121–4 are wanting.

The same poem attributed to Brampton is in MS. Trin. R. 3. 20, p. 197.

2. One leaf of a prose preface to the fifteen Oo's of St. Bridget: imperfect at both ends.   18

And xv⁰ ryghtwyse men of hys kyn shall be kepte in good lyfe

—a hydowys crye ryght as alle that was in the wood had ben revyn uppe by the

Two faint stamps are on the lower margin of this leaf.

3. A lyrical poem, Peter Idle's Instructions to his Son, in seven-line stanzas.   The headline is Pers, or Peris, Ideley.   19

Begins imperfectly (with stanza 8).   Stanzas 1–50 ed. by Miessner, *Peter Idle*, Greifswald, 1903.   Carleton Brown, no. 935.

> Late not thy tonge clak as a mylle
> Medyl not off eche manys mater
> Kepe wᵗin thy brest that myght be stylle
> In tavernys also ne clap ne clater
> Ne wade not so depe in to the water
> But thou may come out at thy plesour
> And not to abyde thyne enmys leysour.

Ends imperfectly, 43ᵇ :

> And he that wolnot repent of hys mysdede
> And make a sethe or he go hens to dye
> To helle he gothe wᵗ sorowe & drede
> Wher ys grontyng of tethe and oryble cry
> And ther contenvally to abyd and ly
> Woth owȝt redemcyown in any maner kynde
> And ther to dwelle woth owȝty any ende.

A comparison with the University Library MS. Ee. 4. 37, shows that little is wanting at the beginning or end of this first part, but that the gaps are many.

The second part of the poem is in the main a modernized version in seven-line stanzas of Robert de Brunne's *Handlyng Synne*.   44

The headline is at first *The Comaundementis*.

It begins imperfectly in the story of the Tempted Monk (cf. *Handlyng Synne*), ed. Furnivall, Roxburghe Club, p. 7, l. cir. 171).   On the First Commandment :

> And playnely to say yowe as it was
> The monke went thane fro hys selle
> And forsoke hys abyt and hys plase
> And dede as I schall yowe telle
> he folowyd hys enemye the devyll of hell
> And went in to egypte in þat contre
> And enabyte hym there in a fayre cete.

(= Furnivall. He was so temptyd wyþ lecherye
> He ȝede fro hys celle to seke folye
> He dede hym sone to a cyte
> In to Egypte þat yche cuntre.)

The next example, f. 50ᵇ, is that of the Witch and her Cow-sucking Bag = Furnivall, p. 17, l. 501, which is peculiar to Robert of Brunne as compared with his French original, William of Wadington (Manuel des Péchés).

The Second Commandment begins f. 52ᵇ.

A gap after f. 54 : the end of the Second and beginning of the Third Commandment are given.

The Third Commandment, f. 55.

The Fourth, 59ᵇ.

The Fifth, 64ᵇ.

The Sixth, 69.

The Seventh, 80 ; f. 83 mutilated.

A gap after f. 89, where were the end of the Seventh and the beginning of the Eighth.

The Eighth, 90.

The Ninth, 93ᵇ.

The Tenth, 94ᵇ.

A gap after f. 94 has carried away the end of this and the beginning of the Seven Deadly Sins. The headline after this is *Synnys*.

Begins imperfectly in *Pride*.

95

> I report me yf nowe vsed be eny pryde inordenate
> Never more I trowe sythe god was borne
> And that in every degre & eche maner of astate
> ffyrst to be gynne at þe hedes þe here ys not shorne.

On 97ᵇ is the tale of the Knight who loved new fashions = Furnivall, p. 107.

On 99ᵇ, the Proud Lady = Furnivall, p. 103.

(On 100ᵇ is a shield with a merchant's mark, and
> Ma. Booth anᵒ aetat. 82. 1674.)

After 100 is a gap. The beginning of *Anger* gone.

Anger begins in the tale of the Merciful Knight (Furnivall, p. 121).

Envy, 102ᵇ (a merchant's mark in the initial).

A merchant's mark on 106ᵇ ; f. 107 mutilated.

A gap after 106ᵇ : most of *Envy* and the beginning of *Sloth* lost.

Sloth, 107. A gap after 107.

A gap after 116. The end of *Sloth* and beginning of *Avarice* lost.

Avarice, 117 ; f. 120 mutilated. Several gaps.

Gluttony, 123ᵇ ; f. 126 upper half gone. 130 mutilated.

Lechery, 133. The hand changes.

Ends imperfectly 134ᵇ :

> The seconde fynger ys the towchnyge
> .   .   .   .
> But inwerde slethe be hert and wylle
> And thou touche pyche it clevyth stylle.

There is some curious ornament in the book in the form of coloured initials and partial borders : at the top and bottom of the pages the tails of letters are apt to be prolonged into flourishes which are decked with couples of short red lines crossing them at intervals. The flourishes at top are more elaborate.

On 45ᵇ is scribbled, Mr Spragene and masteres spragen.

On 78ᵃ : tyme of Kinge henry the viijᵉ by me hovmfri pawer. . . .

On 128ᵇ : Robart cllarke.

NEW TESTAMENT IN ENGLISH.
C.M.A. 6751. 32.   [2073.]

Vellum, $10\frac{9}{10} \times 7\frac{1}{2}$, ff. 351, double columns of 30 lines. Cent. xv, fairly early (*cir.* 1440, Forshall and Madden). In a fine large hand, with excellent ornaments.

The beautiful binding is of the same type as that of 15, 16, and 1603, but with differences of colouring, and not so well preserved. The fore-edges are gilt and marbled.

Collation: 1^8-42^8 43^2 (1 canc. 2 a fragment) 44^8 45^6.

The New Testament in the more recent Wycliffite version. No. 123 in Forshall and Madden.

The order of books is :
The Gospels with prologues.
Pauline Epistles. Laod. (without prol.) follows Col. The rest have prologues.
The Ep. to the Laodiceans is in a peculiar version found only here, and printed by F. and M., vol. iv, p. 438.
Acts, with prol. Cath. Epp. (with one prol.).
Apocalypse with prologue.
Here eendeþ þe apocalips of Joon þe laste book of þe newe testament And bigynneþ þe lessouns and pistlis of þe olde lawe þᵗ ben red in þe chirche in al þe ʒeer after þe uss of saliburi.   286ᵇ
þe firste fridai pistil in aduent Isaie. li. chapitle.
The last is for the feast of Relics.
Here eendiþ þe dominicals and ferials togidere of al þe ʒeer.   323ᵇ
Now bigynneþ þe rule of þe sanctorum both propre & comon̄ togidere (Andrew to Katherine).
Here eendiþ þe sanctorum boþe þe propre & comyn togidere and here bigynneþ þe temporal þat is þe commemoraciouns of þe ʒeer (really the Common of Saints ending with the alternative for a Virgin Martyr).   334ᵇ
f. 337, blank on the verso, is all cut away except the half column which is written.
Here bigynneþ a rule þat telleþ in whiche chapitirs of þe bible ʒe mai fynde þe lessouns pistles & gospels þat ben red in þe chirche after þe uss of Salisburi, etc.
Ending f. 357ᵇ (with Missae votivae, called the Temporal).
Thus eendiþ þis kalender of lessouns pistlis & gospels of al þe ʒeer.
Each book has a beautiful initial in bright colours on gold ground : of fine English work. Smaller initials are uniformly in blue with red flourishing.

At top of f. 336ᵇ is
Praye for the soll of my Lord Wyllm̄ Weston & all cri*sti*an.
On 338ᵇ in the same hand : Rodrot (or -rok).
On 351ᵇ lined through :
All you maisters that hath affexcion to Rede vppon this bowk at your
bygynyng praye for the soll of Sʳ Wylliam Weston lord of senct Johans
Jerusalem in England [of] the which Lord desessithe the viᵗʰ daye of Maye
in the yere of oure Lord god 1540 of whos soll Jhesu haue mercy & all
cri*sti*an solles. Amen.

G. R.

On *l.* is added : Paternoster Ave Crede.
On f. 338 at top is written : This booke was gyven me Edm: Randolph
xxiii die martii 1607 by my frend Sʳ Robert Cotton knighte.
There is also a sketch of a shield bearing a cross with five stars.
On 338ᵇ the names of Edmond Herenden & Thomas Bache (xvi–xvii)
are written several times.

MISCELLANEOUS TRACTS.

C.M.A. 6736, 21. (no. 5), 6738. 23. (no. 7), 6809. 90. (no. 12).
[**2099.**]

Paper, $11\frac{1}{10} \times 7\frac{1}{2}$, pp. 234, in various hands of Cent. xvii. The sides
are covered with purple paper, patterned with black and gold.

There is a table of contents made for Pepys, in which the dates of the
documents are usually specified.

	Year.	Pag.
1 Lᵈ Cecills Advice to his Son (Robert).	1612	1
2. Lᵈ Coventrys Will.	1639	4
(26 July 1638.)		
3. Tho: Killegrew's Letter of his Travels.	1635	10
(Orleans 7 Dec. 1635 N. S.)		
Other copies at Trinity College, Dublin, etc.		
4. The D: of Buckinghams Unhappy Expedition to the	1627	26
French Islands. Secretly discovered by W: ff: an		
unfortunate Commander in that untoward service.		
By W. Fleetwood. Somer's Tracts, ed. 1750, II. 2.		
p. 465.		
5. Bp. Williams's Grievances in the Star-Chamber.		37
Various other tracts are specified in the heading.		
6. Bp. Moreton's (of Durham) Confession (of Faith).	1658	82
See Barwick's *Life*, p. 127.		

	Year.	Pag.
7. Hobbes's Elements of Law Natural and Politick.	1640	84

Ed. from MSS. by Ferdinand Tönnies, 1889.

8, 9. Audland the Quaker's Letter to Prinn.   174

Prinn's Answer thereto.   179

Printed 1672.

10. Coll. Gounter's (Gunter's) Relacion of the King's

    Escape from Worcester.   1651   183

11. Sr Lionel Jenkins's Will.   1685   191

12. Rentale D^{ni} Archiepiscopi Cantuariensis, imperfect.   210

This is the oldest document in the volume. Part of it is dated in 25 Henry VIII and appears to be of that time.

HOCCLEVE.
    C.M.A. 6789. 70.   **[2101.]**

Vellum, $11\frac{1}{5} \times 7\frac{7}{10}$, ff. 83, 28 lines to a page. Cent. xv. In a rather current hand, with good ornament.

The sides are covered with purple paper patterned with gold : lettered. Poem on K. Hen. VI. Manuscript.

Collation : gap | 1^8–3^8 (wants 8) 4^8 5^8 (wants 5) 6^8–11^8 (wants 6–8).

Hoccleve's Regement of Princes.

(Cf. E.E.T.S. text, ed. by Furnivall, 1897.)

Begins imperfectly at l. 449
    Also ther is another newe

ll. 1737–92 (one leaf) are wanting after f. 23.

ll. 2465–99 (one leaf) are wanting after f. 35.

Ends imperfectly with l. 5208 :
          he lefte pees in erthe truly.

The complete poem with the Envoy contains 5463 lines.

There are good borders and initials at ff. 28, 30^b, 44^b, 50, 52^b, 55^b, 60^b, 62^b, 64^b, 65^b, 75^b, 77^b, 80^b.

There are some late scribbles on margins : the name of Henry Caswall occurs on f. 44.

On 62 My lady Coley (?).

On 63^b Thomas Coppley.

There are others which I cannot make out.

DEVOTIONAL TREATISES BY HAMPOLE, ETC.
    C.M.A. 6763. 44.   **[2125.]**

Vellum and paper, $11\frac{3}{10} \times 7\frac{9}{10}$, ff. 2+145+1, 30 lines to a page. Cent. xv (not late). In a clear hand.

The old boards are covered with leather on which is Pepys' stamp.

Collation: a^2 1^{12} 2^{12} 3^{14}: A (ten: gap after 5) B^{18} C^{10} D^{12}–G^{12} (wants 6, 8, 9, 10) H^{12} (wants 11, 12^1) I^{16} (wants 16) b^1.

On the fly-leaf ii^b in a late hand rather faint, are notes on the six ages of the world and the coming of the Britons.

Quires 1–3 are of vellum.

1. Title written in cent. xvii or xviii.

The Chastysing of God's Children. Printed in fol. Maunsell's Catalogue.

In drede of *Almyghty god* Religious *frend* (written here and elsewhere over erasure) a short pistill y sende yow of the matter of temptaciouns.

Cap. 1 begins: *Vigilate et orate*, etc. Wakyth and prayeth that ȝe falle nat in to temptacioun.

Ends f. 28^a: ryhtful & mercyful in his ryhtwys chastisyng haue mercy on vs synful. Amen.

2. Meditations on the Passion.

Here begynneth the meditacioun of cristes passioun.

Ho that euer fully desireth to haue ioye in the passion.

Ends 38^b with: Meditacioun of the songe in the free prisone of helle.

Lefteth vp ȝowre hertys

—and stey vp to the souereyn heuene aboue to the whiche he brynge vs that deyed for vs. Amen.

II. 3. Paper: the first leaf rewritten, apparently; it is in a different hand from the rest.

Dimitte me domine ut plangam paululum dolorem meum

—terram miserie et tenebrarum, etc. 39

These bethe the wordis of the holy mon Job in the persone of a synner bewaylyng hys synfull lyffe byfore passed. Dere frend these beth the wordis of the foresayd Job. . . .

Ends 58^b: þorwe þe help grace & mercy of our lord Ihesu crist þ^t is in heuene w^t owte ende. Amen.

4. A short informacioun of contemplatif lif, likned to Marye. 51

I fynde as y rede by doctours & holy mennys writynges þ^t twey maner lyfynges be heere in þis wordle

A short informacioun of Actif lif, likened to þe lyuyng of Marthe. 55^b

Actif lif is ful merytory

—Nowe þus to lyue god graunte vs alle of his grete mercy. Amen.

5. Here bygynneth a fourme of a general confession. Wyth special synnes ȝif a man fynde hym greuyd in any of hem. 58^b

Lauamini et mundi estote. Be ȝe wasshe & be ȝe clene.

—Be ȝe wasshe, etc. . . . mundi estote.

6. " The Mirror." Change of ink : not certainly change of hand. 60ᵇ
Here bygnneth materes of ʒouþe & of age & of vertues & of vices wyth
her kyndely condicions.
The Mirror of Mankind.
Howe mankynde doþ bygynne. Is wonder to discryue so

Wᵗ oute synne þider to wende ; Wᵗ loue to se his faire face. Amen.
Printed by Furnivall, *Hymns*, etc. E.E.T.S., p. 58, from the Lambeth
MS. 853, in which another stanza is added at the end.
Carleton Brown, no. 779.
Prayer. Summe sacerdos et vere pontifex ecce accedo hodie ad
sacramentum corporis tui percipiendum (12 lines).   65
7. Late title : R. Wimbledon his Sermon at Pauls Crosse 1388 in the
Raigne of Henry the 4 on Luke 16. v. 2. Printed by John Charlwood,
1588 in 8ᵛᵒ & diuers times since.   65ᵇ
Redde racionem villicacionis tue. luc. 16. Mi dere frendes ʒe shulleþ
vnderstonde þᵗ Crist Ihesu autor & doctor of trewþe
—and he graunte ous þere of þis Joye part. Amen.
Sermo Thǫme Wymbeldone london predicat. ad crucem in cimiterio
eccl. S. Pauli.
8. Story of the Cross.   73ᵇ
Adam oure former fader whenne he was put out of Paradys

In þis manere as y haue told. crist of his grete mercy wolde þe oure
redempcioun sholde come fro þe same place & of þe same tre wherof &
of whuche fruyt cam first oure dampnacioun.
9. Memoriale de ligno crucis I. C. d. n. ll. 1–70 out of 154.   76ᵇ
Carleton Brown, no. 1082.
Ihesu þᵗ hast me dere y bouʒt. Writ now gostly in my þouʒt.
Ends imperfectly : Ihesu þᵗ art so mychel of myʒt. Writ in myn herte.
10. Of the Mercy of God.
Seynt barnabe þe apostle seyth of þe mercy of oure lord god þus. In
owr lord good þer be two grete prowesses of hys wonderful mildenesse.
On ys þᵗ he pacyently abideþ þe trespassour. An oþer ys þᵗ he mercy-
fully receuyþ ys repentaunt. This ys þe dowble swetnesse of charite þᵗ
abowndeth in þe brest of oure lord Ihesu crist. Longnesse in abidynge
& lightnesse in forʒyuyng, etc.
—And riʒt so after þis lif þer may no man be recounsiled.
11. (Of contemplation.)   80ᵇ
A gret clerke þᵗ men clepen Richard of seynt Victores settyþ in a booke
þᵗ he made of contemplacōn.
— y rede þᵗ þᵘ lerne hit at seynt luke in his gospell.

Missus est Angelus Gabriel.
Not the text in Horstmann, *Hampole*, i. 162.
12. Of þe manere of lyuyng of oure lady Marie. 82ᵇ
Of oure gloriouse lady Marie maiden moder & wyf.
From the revelations of Elizabeth of Schönau, & St. Jerome de nativitate
B.V.M.
—þu may fynde in þe legende of hir natiuite. þe ioye of hem ȝif vs
god. Amen.
Horstmann, l.c., i. 158.
13. De paciencia. A paragraph. 83ᵇ
Deere frend ho may more esily bere a gret burthen.
Verses: dialogue between Christ on the Cross and the Virgin (8). 83ᵇ
Mater. quid nate. Cur fles. Quia segregor a te.

. . . . .

Cui nichil equale virgo maria vale.
14. A postyle. 84
Sikerly y knowe no þyng þᵗ so inwardly shal take þyn herte to coueyte
god is loue
Epistola supra hortatur relinquere vana huius mundi et adherere
celestibus.
15. Of þre þyng(*is*) þᵗ bryngen (a) man þᵗ is in dedly synn(e) to
helle. 84
In euery a synful man or womman þᵗ is bowndyn in dedly synne
—he may do no more þan god ȝiveþ hym leue for to do.
See below on 21.
16. A good rule for men þᵗ desireþ to lyue perfit lif. 85ᵇ
þe comaundement of god is þt we loue oure lord god
—when þey haue loued. to þᵗ ioye he bryng vs. Amen.
Horstmann, *Hampole*, i. 61.
17. The Seven Joys of the Virgin. 88ᵇ
Legitur quod cum b. Thomas Cantuar. Archiep. septem gaudia
—in gloria perpetuo mecum gauisurum.
Proverbs and verses, English and Latin. Carleton Brown, no. 849 (only
this copy cited).
> If a thought come to thyn herte
> to do or seye in ony degre,
> Be nat to hastyf lest þu smerte
> til þu riȝt wel avised be, etc.
18. The Charter of the Abbey of the Holy Ghost. (Printed by Winkyn
de Word, Maunsell Cat.) 89
Þys bok spekith of þe abbey of þe holy gost.
Printed by Horstmann, *Hampole*, i. 327.

—þ^t for loue of mannes sowle died on þe rode tre.   Amen (ter).
Thus endith þe abbey of the holigost.

19. A meditacōn how a man shal gouerne hym in the tyme þ^t he
heeryth his masse.   97
   for þis sacrament offreþ holy churche
—þenne lat þyn herte be ocupyed in þe maner as hit is forseyd &
wryten.
Prayers to St. Anne, All Saints, the Virgin.   (Latin.)   98^b
On hearing the gospel *In principio.*   (Latin.)
Scriptum repperi quod b. Joh. Euuang. postquam b. Maria assumpta erat
in celum desiderauit eam videre.   (She tells Christ of her seven sorrows.)
—Et qui per septimanam te rogauerit dabo tibi animam illius ut facias
cum ea secundum voluntatem tuam.

20. Hic inc. tres gradus amoris sec. Ric. de Hampol.   99
Ego dormio et cor meum vigilat.   Þu þ^t lusteth to loue bowe down þyn
eere
   Containing: Oracio de passion in verse.   101
      Haf mynde vpon þi kyng.   how he þe water wepte.
Ends: Þ^t loue Ihesus vs graunte.   Amen.
Horstmann, *Hampole*, i. 49.   Carleton Brown, no. 693.
Yf þ^t wult lyue perfetly keep þis short rewle here folowyng.   102
   Do al þyn entent to do goddes wille.
On: The seuen workes of mercy bodili.   102
21. Inc. tract. Ricardi Hampol heremite de conuersione ad deum et
eius amore (title in other ink and perhaps another hand).   102^b
In euery man & womman þ^t is bounden, etc.
See above, f. 84.   This second copy ends with the same words (for to
do), f. 105, and this note follows in the hand of the later.
Quere residuum superioris istius tractatus in quinto folio subsequente.
Et inc. sic.
   ffor þu hast forsake þe ioye, etc.
Hampole's *Forma Viuendi.*   Horstmann, *Hampole*, i. 1.
22. Meditation: Thenk man what þu hast ben & what þu art.   105
Containing day and night prayers.
   —Suffre paciently þ^t men sey þe þow hit be vntrewe.
23. Here bygynneþ a meditacōn þ^t þu shall þenk certayn houres of þe
day & first *hora matutina.*   106^b
   Byfore matyns þu shalt þenke on cristes natiuite
      —as doþ dropes of water fro an hows after a showr of reyn.
In þe lif of seynt Bernard hit is wryten þ^t þe deuell seide.   108^b
(The seven verses: *Illumina oculos,* etc.)
Prayer to the four archangels.   108^b

Exemplum de gratia dei : Thow þe sonne shyne on þe hows.   109
24. ffor men & wymmen that beþ enclosed (the continuation of no. 21).   109
For þᵘ hast forsaken þe ioye
—þerof þank god & pray for me þe grace of I. C. be wᵗ þe & kepe þe. Amen.
Omnipotens dominus compleat aliud opus factum.   Richard of Hampol made þis rewle of lyuyng.
25.   Hic inc. quedam oracio quam docuit S. Ursula Johanni heremyte de Warwyk.   116ᵇ
Unum pater noster et credo in honore s. trinitatis, etc.
Et idem heremita notificauit istam precem inter profundos doctores et illi receperunt istam precem dicere in magna reuerencia.
O bone ! O dulcissime ! etc.
Invocations of SS. Achatius Denis George Christopher Blasius Giles Ciricus Katherine Margaret Barbara Martha Julitte.
Orent pro nobis omnes sancte, etc.
26. Meditacio bona (Horstmann, l.c., ii. 441).   117
If hit so be þᵗ þᵘ coueite to be clensed in soule
A gap after 117.
— a special seruice of fifty auees if þᵘ may fre þe & me & alle mankynde.
Et dicat istam salutacionem . . . quadragesies, etc.
Aue maria ⎫
prouida pia ⎬ pro peccatore, etc.
proxima via ⎭
On labels : Sit nomen domini benedictum.
The monogram i h c, written large.   About it : " Ihū miserere.   Amore langueo Ihū mercy.   Ihū amice meus.
Below : Knele down man lat for no shame.   To wurschipe Ihc þi lordes name   sythen angels knelen & deuelis also.   Wel auȝte þe man to knele þerto.   Sit nomen domini bened.   Ex hoc nunc, etc.   Carleton Brown, no. 1129.
Oremus.   Deus cui omne cor patet, etc.
On a frame round three sides : In nomine Ihesu omne genus, etc.
Note of Indulgence of John (xxii) and prayer Anima Christi.   118ᵇ
Qui hanc or. dixerit sequentem contra arma Ihesu Christi (6070 years of indulgence).
Cruci corone spinee Clauisque dire lancee, etc.
Quicunque hec arma d. n. I. C. subsequentia deuote inspexerit (Indulgence).

The following leaf which contained the arms, is torn out, and so are at least two others which had English verse on them.

27. Of þe pater noster.   119
    Ihesu crist in a sermon þ^t he made tauȝte his disciples
      —pes & sikernesse in blisse þ^t is endeles.   Amen (ter).

28. Of faith.   Broþer be stedfast & trewe of bileeue of þi feyþ.   *Sine fide impossibile.*   [124
      —& who so haþ hit verreily he shal be saued sikerly.   Amen (ter).
Change of hand.

29. As witnesyth holy wry^t & holy doctours ther beth two weyes contraryous.   [125^b
      —to þ^t blisse he ous brynge.   Þat of nowȝt made al þyng.   Amen (ter).

30. Here it spekeþ of þre arewes þ^t shulleþ be y shote to hem þat shulleþ be y dampned.   128^b
    Who so wul haue in mynde þe dredful day of dome
      —wiþ his precious blod vpon þe rode hangynge.   Amen (ter).
Horstmann, l.c., ii. 446.

31. Spiritus Guidonis in verse (Carleton Brown, no. 1681, only in this copy).   131
    Oure merueyllous god þ^t most ys of myȝt : alwey he wurcheþ to fastne
      oure fey
    Redily to shewe by gostly lyȝt: to knowe his mercy to man alwey.

     .   .   .   .   .   .

    And graunte vs to lyue as þy wille ys . euere þe while we beþ lyuynge.
                                           Amen.
Expt. reuelacio spiritus Guydonis.
Another English metrical version is printed by Horstmann, *Hampole*, ii. 292.

32. Sermo in die Pasche.   139
    Iesum queritis Nazarenum. . . . Cristen children in god as ye witeþ we þis day ye beþ at þe feste & graunt mawnger of þe kyng of heuene.
Ends f. 143^a.
    & to þe whiche blisse crist brynge vs þ^t for vs shadde his blod.   Amen (ter).
On 143^b is only one line :
Aqua tome quinquies varia(n)s colorem [varia(n)s colorem] in lac semel tra(nsiens ?) et quater in cruorem.

33. On 144 in a later hand :
A deuout doctour of þe churche in an holy contemplacion made for gret encresse of deuocion.
(On the Sorrows of the Virgin.)

—and euery desyre þat ye wol pray me for w(hether) hyt be for your-
selfe or eny of your seruauntes y shall truly performe to your pl(easure).
On the vellum fly-leaf, in the hand of the first fly-leaf:
Prognostics of Esdras in verse (Carleton Brown, no. 720, only in this
copy).

> Here bith the words feire and swete
> that Ihesus schewed Esydras the prophete
> that he ham schulde schewen well
> to the children of Israell
> And of qualite of the yere
> that wollen byfalle euery where, etc.

Ends imperfectly:

> Olde men shullen dede be
> And frutes well growyng & wexyng on (?) tree.

These prognostics (known in later times as *Erra pater*) go back at
least to Greek originals: on which see Tischendorf, *Apocalypses Apocr.*,
Introd.; Bensly, *Missing Fragment of 4th Book of Esdras*, etc., etc.

HERDINGE'S METRICAL CHRONICLE OF ENGLAND.
C.M.A. 6722. 7. [2163.]

Paper, 11½ × 8, ff. 643 written, 34 lines to a page. Cent. xvi. Pretty
clearly and neatly written.
On f. 1. Fairfax 1654: and above this, scribbled over:
Edward Harelay (?? it *might* be Farefax) his booke 1659 (or 1639).
History of England in verse from William Rufus to Henry VIII.
The proper title appears to be The English and French Chronicles.
It begins with William Rufus.

> Wilyam Rufus otherwyes William the Rede
> Whoo was the seconde sonne began for to succede
> Of William the conquerour ouer the realme of Englande
> The ix of Julie & of our compt full a thousande
> And fourescore nine the eleuenth yeare not to skippe
> Of the ffrennche kinge than reigninge the first Pilippe.

ff. 14ᵇ 15ᵃ blank.
The first division is at f. 33, in Stephen's reign:
Thus endes the firste booke off the ffourthe volume of the Englisshe &
ffraunche Cronicles.
Book II is marked as ending both at f. 91 and f. 139; Book III at 267;
Book IV at 358. This has the Envoy headed: Herdinges Lenuoy:

> O mercifull god what ane prince was this.

Book V ends at 452.

Book VI has the end marked and crossed out at 481.

The text ends in 38 Henry VIII:

> To y^{er} great displeasure, then the ffrenche kynge haistely
> Caused the worke to be defaced lest kynge henrye should be
>   angury.

Finis.

On 643 is:

Ane Lenuoy to his iiij volumes

in six seven-line stanzas.

> Yow Comydes & Tragides; me recommend
> Unto the learned & unlittered also

etc.; ending:

> Amonge thinges remembre as thynge most necessary
> The high falle of ye Archebishoppe Cardynall Wolsy.

The earlier portion is a versification of Fabyan's Chronicle, which ends with Richard III (ed. of 1516). There are frequent references to Fabyan in the text. The English renderings of Latin verses which occur are taken bodily from him. I have not succeeded in finding who Herdinge was: he is not John Hardynge, the author of the rhymed Chronicle. I take him to have been the compiler of the whole of this enormous book.

HOWARD'S DEFENCE OF THE REGIMENT OF WOMEN.
C.M.A. 6737. 22.   [2191.]

Paper, $11\frac{7}{10} \times 7\frac{7}{10}$, ff. 220, 39 lines to a page. Cent. xvi. Very neatly written within borders of red lines.

A dutifull defence of the lawfull Regiment of Women deuided into three bookes. The first conteyneth reasons & examples grounded on the law of nature. The second reasons & examples grounded on the ciuile lawe. The third reasons & examples grounded on the sacred lawes of god with an awnswer to all false and friuilous obiections wch haue bene most vniustly countenaunced with deceitfull coulores forced oute of their lawes in disgrace of their approued & sufficient aucthorytie. 1

Dan. 13. 57. Sic faciebatis filiabus Israel et illae timentes loquebantur vobis sed Filia Iuda non sustinuit iniquitatem vestram.

On 1^b are the arms of Cecil emblazoned in colour with crest and supporters and motto: *Cor unum via una.* With these lines:

Ut Leo maturas segetes suffulcit in aruis
　Cecilius messem seruat alitque domi.
Vtilis est patriae iustus facilisque querenti
　Eloquar expertus quod retulere probi
Non Sirtis non Silla vorax non vasta Charibdis
　Emeriti poterit tollere facta viri
Vt deus ergo tuam stirpem cumulauit honore
　Sic tua perpetuo flumine fata riget.
Nestoris ingenium tibi qui largitur et artes
　Longaeui tribuat tempora laeta senis.

Tuae D in perpetuum deuinctiss.

H. Hωward.

To the Queenes most excellent Maiestie.　　　　　　　2

It pricketh now fast vpon the point of thirtene years most excellent . . . since the copie of a railing inuective against the regiment of queenes in generall . . . was deliuered to mee by an honorable priuy Councellor, etc.

This dedication, which contains a good deal of autobiographical matter, ends on f. 27 with the author's signature.

Book I begins f. 28 :

It may seeme strange to men of grounde & knowledge.

Book II, 125^b.

Book III, 154.

Ending f. 219^a :

and that hir comfortable goverment wch began wth hope maie end wth happynesse.　Sanctae et indiuiduae trinitati sit omnis honor laus et gloria in saec. saec. amen.

The book seems to have been completed in 1582 : it has not been printed.　There are other MS. copies of it, e. g. in Harley 7021 (art. 11).

CHRONICLE ROLL.

C.M.A. vac.　　　　　　　　　　　　　　　　　**[2244.]**

Vellum roll protected by book-covers, about 14 ft. long by 8⅘ in. broad. Cent. xv, late.　Fairly well written.

Chronicle Roll in English.

Consyderyng the grete desyre of many men that wulde haue knowleche of olde croneclys of kynges that afore tyme reigned yn this lande, etc.

Adam was made in damascene ffeld, etc.

A large medallion at top, inscribed *Adam Eua.*

The Biblical genealogy is carried down to the birth of Christ, parallel with that of the kings of Britain from Brutus.　After that the British (and English) line is the only one given.

G

The last note gives the date of the coronation of Edward IV :
The eight and twenti day of Junij in the yere off oure lord*e* a thousand ffoure hundrid sexti & one.
The genealogy ends with Edward IV's six children :
Elizabeth, May, Cecilli, Edward prince, Margarete, Richard.
The reverse is blank.

PILGRIMAGE OF MAN.
C.M.A. 6797. 78.   [2258.]

Paper, 12$\frac{1}{10}$×7$\frac{3}{10}$, ff. 165 written, 30 lines to a page.   Cent. xvii, fairly early.   In a good clear sloping hand; with drawings in pen and ink coloured in water-colour; some fluid gold is used; on the fly-leaf a seal, and a shield drawn in pen and ink; both bear these arms: *arg.* (?), a cross ⳩ fitchee *sable*, a chief indented *or* ⋁⋁⋁.   Above, the initials R. P. (?)

The Pilgrime, or The pilgrimage of Man in this world, wherein the authore plainely and truly setts fourth the wretchedness of man's life in this world without grace oure sole protector.
Written in the yeare of Christ 1331. pag. 4 & 58.

To them of this world which have non House, but short being, and are (as sayth St Pawle) pilgrimes : be they Kings, be they queenes, be they Rich, be they poore, be they strong, be they weake, etc.
Now come neere & gather you together all good ffolke, etc.
Now vnderstand the Dreame that I had the other night in my Bedd as I lay in the Abby.
Cap. 29 ends : And so liue that dying he may dye the death of the righteous, and obtaine a place in the faire Citty of Jerusalem which place god grant vs all both quick & dead.   Amen.
Heere ends the Romance of the Monke which he wrote of the Pilgrimage of the Life of the Manhoode which he made for the good pilgrims of this wordle that they may keepe such way as may bring them to the ioys of Heauen.   Pray for him y^t made it & gratis writt it for the loue of good Christians in the yeare one thousand three Hundred thirty & one.
Finis.

The pictures, one to each chapter, of oblong form, a little broader than the text, illustrate the following subjects :
1. The monk preaching to an audience mostly seated on benches, out of doors.
2. Grace Dieu crowned shows him her house, with water about it.
3. Grace Dieu addresses people : on *r.* a master (monk) making ointments at a table.
4. A man and woman join hands before a mitred official.

5. Moses (?) mitred clips the hair of a kneeling monk : a number of others look on.
6. Reason preaching to an audience.
7. Moses administers the Eucharist to kneeling people.
8. People on *l.* Penitence with rod, and besom in her mouth. Charity with book. Moses on *r.*
9. Charity speaks : Moses on *l.*, people on *r.* in white.
10. Grace Dieu shows the pilgrim an open box in which are staff and scrip.
11. He holds the staff (Burdon) she handles the scrip.
12. Drawing aside a curtain she shows him gold and silver armour.
13. The pilgrim and Reason meet a great churl with a club (Rude-entendment).
14. Reason (?) on *r.* The pilgrim in *c.* Memory holding armour on *l.*
15. The pilgrim and Reason (?) on *l.* Idleness reclining : above her, Labour weaving a mat.
16. The pilgrim. On *l.* a woman who has caught his foot in a chain.
17. Flattery on all fours with a mirror. Pride on her back with a horn and a club. Pilgrim and Reason on *r.*
18. Envy on all fours : Treson and Detraction on her back. Pilgrim on *r.*
19. The pilgrim overthrown by four women. Wrath on *l.* with club, and scythe at girdle.
20. The pilgrim. Avarice with six arms and two stumps, holding balance, cup, sun, etc.
21. By another hand : Woman on *l.* holds an anvil to her mouth. *Gula* on *r.* mounted on a boar.
22. The first hand : Grace Dieu shows the pilgrim an eye in the rock, whence water flows.
23. He stands by water in which are people, two of them clothed and winged. A devil on the horizon.
24. Carrying a flowering spray he is borne on the back of a man through the air.
25. Standing on the shore : a great ship (Religion) in the sea.
26. Grace Dieu shows him a great cloistered court with people walking in it.
27. He kneels. Obedience binds his hands.
28. He is attacked by two women, one on crutches.
29. He lies in bed. The two women at the foot. Death, a skeleton with scythe, stands on the bed. Grace Dieu at the head.

These pictures are not close copies of mediaeval originals. Probably the subjects and compositions may follow old models : but the architecture, for instance, is that of cent. xvi or xvii. With the exception of no. 21, which is quite poor, they are not unskilfully done.

The text is a condensed version of the *Pélerinage de vie humaine*, by Guillaume de Deguileville, monk of Châlis (oise). A full English version was printed for the Roxburghe Club by W. Aldis Wright, M.A. (*Pilgrimage of the Lyf of the Manhode*) in 1869. Mr. Wright refers on p. x of his Preface to a manuscript in the University Library, Ff. 6.30, with exactly the same title as ours. The colophon is :

"Written according to yͤ first copy. The originall being in St Johns Coll. Oxford, & thither given by Will. Laud Archbp. of Canterbury who had it of Will. Baspoole, who, before he gave to the Archbp. the originall, did copy it out. By which it was verbatim written by Walter

Parker, 1645, and from thence transcribed by G. G. 1649. And from thence by W. A. 1655."

The Laudian MS. is now in the Bodleian (Laud Misc. 740), but it is a copy of the older and full version.

For specimens of other illustrations of this book see *The Ancient Poem of G. de Guileville . . . edited from notes collected by the late Mr. Nathaniel Hill*, etc. Pickering 1858.

CHRONICLE ROLL (ST. AUGUSTINE'S, CANTERBURY).
C.M.A. 6721. 6.   [2314.]

Vellum roll, folded and bound in a cover. 8⅜ in. broad and about 20 ft. long. Cent. xv, *cir.* 1450. Finely written.

The extreme top of the roll, torn away in old times, has been restored with great skill and neatness. The heading and parts of 3–5 lines were gone.

The main subject of the roll is the succession of the Archbishops of Canterbury. It is thus arranged, from *l*:

Anni domini from 597 to 1550.

Pontifices Romani from Gregory the Great to Eugenius IV (1430).

Kings of England and their children: beginning with Reges Cantiae (Ethelbert, etc.) and proceeding with Kings of England to Henry VI.

Archbishops of Canterbury from Augustine to Henry (I) Chichele (1415).

Years of the coming of Augustine: 1 to 954 (= 1550 A.D.).

Indictio (so restored in the heading, but apparently the Sunday letter.)

Aureus numerus.

The Kings are distinguished by a gold crown and a verse in red.
That for Ethelbert is:

Rex etelbertus primus stat honore repertus.

Edbald: Edbaldi regis violencia fit via legis.
Alfred: Oxoniis flores Alured fert rite priores.

Henry VI has three crowns, and the following verses:

Wyndesore henrici fulgens quit origine dici
Anno qui stema tulit octauo dyadema.

Below:

Lilia quamcicius francorum celica dona
Rexit. parisius fuit huic geminata corona.

The last person entered in the genealogy is:

Margareta filia et heres ducis Somerset . . . per regem in matrimonium Iohanni filio et heredi Willelmi Marchionis Suff.[1]

[1] This is the Lady Margaret, Countess of Richmond and Derby, who was born in 1441.

There are a good number of notes of historical events: the last few are:

1417   Burning of Sir John Oldcastle.

1421   Birth of Henry VI.

1422   Deaths of Henry V and Charles VI of France.

John Duke of Bedford made regent of France.

Bellum de creuant contra Armoricatos et Scotos.

Bellum de verneul ou perche contra armoros et scotos deuictos per Ioh. regentem francie ducem bedford xvii^us Aug.

1431   Council of Basel.

1435   Obitus dux bedford' Regens regni franc' die sancte crucis septembris.

The rest being blank except for the entries of dates which are carried down to 1550.

The Archbishops' column begins thus: Augustinus venit in angliam (restored).

603. Pallium (? mittitur) augustino. Ordinacio melliti et justi.

606. Orbitus (!) Augustini. Laurencius.

At 822. Translatio sepulture archiepiscoporum contra decretum S. Augustini per suggestionem Wilfredi archiep. ad ecclesiam Christi cui fauit baltredus Intrusor qui statim postea expulsus fuerat per egbertum regem Westsaxonum.

At 911. Note of the foundation of the Cluniac order.

At 1074. Foundation of the Priory (Cluniac) of Lewes.

1119. S. Thomas londoniencis nascitur. His martyrdom and translation also noted.

At 1282-4. Death of Llewellyn and: Corona regis arthuri inuenta est que apud Wall' magno honore fuit et domini (!) regi oblata.

There are no entries about Canterbury buildings. The note for the year 822 quoted above betrays a connexion with St. Augustine's Abbey. And, in fact, a comparison of this roll with the similar table prefixed to Thomas of Elmham's unfinished History of the Abbey of St. Augustine, edited by Hardwick in the Rolls Series (*Hist. Mon. St. Aug. Cant.*) shows that the roll is not independent of that work. The method of reckoning by years of St. Augustine is common to both. Various notes, e.g. that on Pope Joan, agree word for word; and some small events, e.g. the siege of Leeds Castle (Kent) in 1320, are recorded in both. Moreover the fact that Thomas of Elmham became a Cluniac accounts for the mention of the Cluniacs and of Lewes, which was their first home in England.

The general style of the writing closely resembles that of the manuscript of Elmham at Trinity Hall.

ARITHMETICA JORDANI, ETC. [2329.]
C. M. A. 6767–6776, 6778, 6780–6784.

Vellum, $12\frac{1}{2}\times9\frac{3}{4}$, ff. 224×4, mostly in double columns of 31 lines. Cent. xv, early (1407). Well written.

In two main divisions, of which the first has fine initials added by what I think is an Italian hand.

There are good diagrams, and three excellent "volvels", i. e. moveable diagrams of the spheres, etc., on several layers of discs of paper : bronze, gold, and silver paper are used here. They occur on ff. 64^{b}, 73^{a}, 92^{b}.

The first part of the MS. was written at Paris in 1407 by Servatius Tomlinger, of Munich. It was given to Peterhouse in 1472. In the old register of that College it is entered second among the books given by Roger Marchall (see my Catalogue, p. 23). Leland saw it at Peterhouse (*Collectanea* iv. 21): in 1556 it appears in a list of books borrowed from Peterhouse on 6 May by Dr. John Dee to be returned in 1558. Another book (Ashmole MS. 424), which he borrowed at the same time, was presented to him by Peterhouse in 1564 in exchange for some printed books, and it is likely that our MS. became his property on the same terms. It figures as no. 91 in the list of his MSS. made in 1583. (See my *Lists of MSS. formerly owned by Dr. Dee*, Bibliogr. Soc. 1921, pp. 7, 12, 25). It was in Pepys' possession in 1697 when the *Catalogi MSS. Angliae* was published, and its contents are entered as separate items there (see the heading).

Binding : original, white skin over boards, clasps gone. Rebacked by Pepys and lettered " Pet. House Miscel. MSS." On the second cover is a label protected with horn, inscribed :

> Arithmetica Iordani cum comento
> Theorica planetarum cum arte equandi
> eosdem per instrumentum geometricum
> Tabula Alfonsi cum canone sequente
> Campanus de compoto ecclesiastico cum aliis
> Ex dono magistri Rogeri Marchall.

Collation : 2 fly-leaves left | 1^{13}–15^{12} 16^{8} 17^{12}–19^{12} | 2 fly-leaves.

On the fly-leaf :

> Ad laudem gloriam et honorem domini nostri Ihesu Christi ac beatissime Virginis Marie matris eius et sancti Raphaelis medicorum post deum principis ac monarche qui et medicina dei appellatur. Ego Rogerus Marchall arte medicus collegii huius sancti Petri Cantebr. dudum socius do lego et concedo hunc librum arismetrice Jordani cum aliis collegio antedicto inibi perpetuis carceribus mancipandum ad usum sociorum eiusdem Collegii antedicti.

Then follows a list of contents in Marchall's hand.

Contents:

I. 1. Arithmetica Iordani

Inc. liber primus Iordani de nemore de elementis arismetrice artis.
    Unitas est esse rei per se.

The initial has a shield paly of six *arg.* and *gules.*

The tract consists of text and comment, with marginal diagrams.

Ends: assignare est possibile.

Expl. distinctio decima et per consequens totus liber de elementis arismetrice artis magistri Jordani de nemore scripta parisius per manus seruatii tomlinger de bauaria a^o d^i m^{mo} quadricentesimo septimo 8^a die post festum penthecoustes finitus liber est iste.

2. Inc. Algorismus de integris (Johannis de Sacro Bosco).   45
    Omnia que a primeua rerum origine

Ends: tam in numeris quadratis quam in cubicis.

Expl. algorismus de integris.

3. Inc. Algorismus de minuciis (M^{ri} Joh. de Lineriis).   50

Text. Modum representacionis minuciarum phisicarum et vulgarium demonstrare

Comm. Quia in fraccionibus duo sunt numeri.

Ends: 4^a 9^{arum} 3^a 6^{arum} 2^a et 3^{arum} integer, etc., etc., etc.

Expl. algorismus de minuciis.

4. Inc. theorica planetarum Campani.   54

At top: Theorica planetarum optima cum equatorio eiusdem secundum Campanum.

Primus phylosophie pater principium (?) ipsius negocium in principia tria dispertitur.

In this tract are the best diagrams (astronomical) and the volvels mentioned above.

Ends: quemadmodum de mercurio supra docuimus.

5. Tractatus magnus et utilis de proporcionibus proporcionum mag^{ri} nicholai horesme.   93^b

Omnis rationalis opinio de uelocitate motuum.

Ends: his ergo 4^{tum} capitulum finiatur tu autem domine miserere mei.

Expl. 4^m capitulum de proporcionibus huius tractatus editus (?) a reuerendo mag^{ro} Nicolao horesme (*marg.* al. horem) scriptus per me seruatium (110 *b*).

Two definitions follow, and then a page is left blank for the beginning of the next tract.

6. (Jordanus de commensuratione celestium).   111^b

Begins imperfectly: refert et etiam posterius videbitur.

Ends: et ipse nescio quomodo super hoc iudex decreuit apollo. Expl.

nobilis tractatus mag^{ri} Jordani de nemore de motibus celestibus. Si motus celestes sunt commensurabiles vel non.

    7. Algorismus proporcionum.   128

Algorismus proporcionum, reuerende presul Meldensis Philippe, quem pictagoram dicerem si fas esset credere finem ipsius de reditu animarum

Ends: de quibus determinatum est sufficienter.

Expl. algorismus proporcionum per manus seruacii de monaco.

The Bishop of Meaux who is here addressed is Philippe de Vitry (1351–62). Dee, and the writer in the *Cat. MSS. Angl.*, make " Gervasius " de monaco the author: but he is evidently the Servatius de Bauaria of Art. 1, who is the scribe of all this part of the manuscript.

    8. In a later hand : text and comment : without heading.

Demonstrationes astrolabii.   131

Tres circulos in astrolapsu descriptos

Ends: cetera in glosa presentis libri 2^e propors (*sic*) inuenies.

Expl. demonstrationes astrolabii.

    9. In the same hand as Art. 8.   Tractatus de turketo.   132^b

Inc. turketus et in prima parte de tabula deseruiente equinoctiali.

De omnibus partibus instrumenti quod turketum dicitur primo dicendum est

Ends : sagax lector facile per se inueniret.

Expl. turketus deo gracias factus a. d. 1284 2^a die Jullii in die dominica sole cancri 17, luna 20, aquarii saturno 20, capricorni Joue 21, sagitarii marte 13 virginis Venus 16 leonis mercurii (!) 28 geminorum capitis 12 capricorni ante (?) meridiem (?). Deo gratias.

    II. In a fine hand, written in red, blue, and black.

    10. Tabule Alfonsi olim Regis Castelle illustris.   133

Ending f. 150^a ; f. 150^b is blank.

    11. Canones tabularum Alfonsi Mag^{ri} Johannis de Saxonia.   151

Tempus est mensura motus ut vult aristotiles 4° phisicorum

Ends: idem motus sicut in coniunccionibus planetarum dictum est et sic est finis.

Expl. Canones illustris regis Alfoncii quos Mag^r Johannes Danckow de Saxonia compilauit (158^b)

    12. Canones tabularum primi mobilis mag^{ri} Johannis de Lineriis. 159

An angel nicely drawn with the pen is beside the initial.

Cuiuslibet arcus proposi[ti] sinum rectum inuenire

Ends : vero loco solis qui fuerit in radice 2^e proporcionis (?).

Expl. Canones tabularum primi mobilis et equacionum simul et eclipsium ordinati per mag^{rum} Johannem de Lineriis pictandum (picardum ?) dyoc. Ambianensis.

13. Alkyndus (the table of contents suggests Lincolniensis) de impressionibus aeris. 185

Ad probandam diuersam aeris disposicionem

Ends : et in signis aquosis.

Expl. tractatus Alchindi de disposicione aeris.

14. De utilitate arismetrice per Rogerum bacoñ. 185ᵇ

De vtilitate arismetrice potest sermi per infra scripta penes (?) res huius mundi quilibet (?) ipsa utatur

Ends : 9⁰ venus 10⁰ luna 11⁰ mercurius.

Et sic est finis huius operis Mʳⁱ Rogerii bakonis ut patet in sua summa ad Clementem.

From Part IV of the *Opus Majus*, ed. Bridges, i. 224–36.

See Little in *Roger Bacon: Commemorative Essays*, Oxford, 1914, p. 382.

15. Compotus magistri Campani. 188

Rogauit me unus ex hiis quibus contradicere nequeo ut scienciam quam compotum appellamus

Ends: istorum vigilias ieiunes luceque Marci.

Expl. compotus bonus Campani.

16. In another good hand.

Algorismus demonstratus per Jordanum ut creditur. 219

Figure numerorum sunt ix. s. 1·2·3·4·5·6·7·8·9 et est prima unitatis

Ends : que suffragantur ad hoc opus (224ᵇ).

The leaf has a catchword *textus*, but the tables of contents show no sign of mutilation.

On the fly-leaf is another table of contents, not in Marchall's hand.

LEGENDARY IN ENGLISH.

C.M.A. 6759. 40. [**2344.**]

Vellum, 12⅖ × 8⅖, ff. 1 + 265, 47 lines to a page. Cent. xiv, early. In brown ink : apparently in two hands, both good.

Collation : 1 fly-leaf; 1⁸ 2⁸ (wants 4, 5) 3⁸–5⁸ (1 canc.) 6⁸ 7⁴ 8⁸ 9⁸ (3 canc.) 10⁸–18⁸ 19⁶ 20⁴ 21⁸–23⁸ (wants 4, 5) 24⁸–26⁸ 27⁶ 28⁸–30⁸ 31⁶ 32 (four left : 2 and 3 fragments) 33⁶ (or eight, wanting 4, 5) 34⁸ 35⁸ 36⁶ 37⁸ (5, 6, 8 canc. or wanting).

On the fly-leaf: recto, at top (xvii). 28

The Legend of the Saints in old English verse.

A charm containing the names of the Three Kings, the name Ananizatta (Ananizapta), etc.

Receipt. To sle wormys in man or childe.

Note.   Annus viii et ix R. h. viij.

Other receipts.

On the verso:

Mem. quod humfredus dux Bukyngham decapitatus fuit apud Bellum Northamt. circa festum translacionis S. Thome Archiep. Cant. anno regni Regis beati Henrici sexti post conquestum xxxix°.

Item (blank) dux Bukingham filius et heres eius humfrᴵ truncatus fuit apud Salesbury in festu commem. animarum anno r. r. Ric. tercii post conq. primo.

Item d. Edwardus dux Bukingham filius et heres eiusd. (blank) truncatus fuit apud Turrim London die veneris xvij die maij in vigil vigilie festi sancte pentecostes anno r. r. Henr. viij post conq. xiij et in die lune prox. preced. condempnabatur apud Westm. per xij dominos et peres regni Anglie coram domino Thoma duce Northfochie ut capital' judice ut traditor suo Regi.

Mem. quod Lambertus filius Thome Aylesbury (lined through) natus fuit xvij° die Sept. in ffesto S. Lamberti Ep. anno r. r. Henr. VIII xviij°.

The same repeated in part.

Aylesbury was the owner of the book in Henry VIII's time, as appears from several other inscriptions.

On 1ᵃ is an original list of contents.

On 1ᵇ xvi early : The names of all my bok*es* at Estret :

> Paraphrasis Erasmi
> Lengenda Sanctorum
> Ovidius cum aliis in uno volumine
> Epistole Caroli Viruli
> Colloquia Erasmi
> Ortus vocabulorum
> An Almynak
> Shepard*es* Callender
> A dictionary
> Encheridion militis christ
> The myrrour of helth
> A treatise of the masse
> A grete volume called Registrum Cronicarum (!)
> A testament in frenche

Another note xv–xvi: ther be leyves in thes booke xiij skore and a vi vij.

The manuscript contains a fairly full Sanctoral of the *South English Legendary*, the various manuscripts of which were being edited for the E.E.T.S. by Dr. C. Horstmann.   I have not at present met with any account of this particular manuscript by him : I refer in my description of it to his edition of the oldest manuscript (Laud 108) which gives the contents of other copies.   There is a full list of contents in Carleton Brown's *Register*, I. 219, and the several articles are indexed in Part II.

The Trinity College manuscript (R. 3. 25) perhaps most nearly resembles ours.

The table of contents in f. 1ᵃ is divided into months and written in

Latin. f. 2 has a border in gold and colour and a small picture in the initial on gold ground of St. Andrew in blue bound to a saltire cross.

1. Heading in red: *Decembʳ. Sanctus Andreas. Legenda sanctorum.*

[p. 1

   St. Andrew. Seint Andrew þe apostle was seint peteres broþer.

2. St. Nicholas, H. p. 240. Seint Nicolas þe goede, man þat goed' confessour was. p. 6

3. St. Lucy, H. p. 101 to l. 148. heuene kyng*e*. Two leaves gone 17

4. St. Thomas Apostle, H. p. 380, l. 143 to end. 21

5. St. Stephen. Seint Steuene was a grew. 27

6. St. John Evangelist, H. p. 402. 29

7. St. Thomas of Canterbury, cf. H. p. 106. Gilbert was seint Thomas ffader name: þat triwe man was & good. 41

   Ends with the Mors militum, H. p. 174.

8. St. Anastasia. Seint Anastase was y bore: at Rome by olde lawe.

[90

9. Euangelium In principio. Among holy gospelles alle: hit is nouȝt goed to byleue.[1] 93

10. Prologue (*Banna Sanctorum*). Now bloweþ þis nywe ffeste: þat late bygan to sprynge.

[97

11. (Circumcision). ȝeres day þe holy ffeste: þat holy ffeste is & goed.

[99

12. Twelfth day. Twelfþe day þe heye ffeste: noble is to holde. 99

13. St. Hilary. Seint Hillari þe holy man 100

14. St. Wlstan, H. p. 67. 102

15. SS. Fabian and Sebastian. Seint ffabian by olde lawe 107

    Seint S. was a man of gret hond 107

16. St. Agnes, H. p. 181. 110

17. St. Vincent, H. p. 184. A leaf lost after p. 116. 114

18. St. Julian, H. p. 255. 117

19. St. Julian Hospitaller, H. p. 256. A leaf lost after p. 118: pp. 119–122 misbound. 118

20. St. Bridget. Seint Bride þe holy mayde of yrlonde was 121

21. St. Blasius, H. p. 485. 125

22. St. Agatha, H. p. 193. 130

23. St. Scholastica, H. p. 197. 133

24. St. Valentine. 134

25. St. Juliana. 135

26. St. Matthias. 140

27. St. Oswald (of York). 141

28. St. Chad. 146

[1] This article is specially notable as of rare occurrence.

Only ll. 1–26 remain, beginning :

> Seint Thomas þe holy man : vnder þe eorþe lay
> Ar he yschryned were : many a long day

ending :

> þat þer com vnder ffonge.

This is the last item in the original list of contents.

There are some curious marginal notes in the book, of cent. xv–xvi.

On p. 203 *inter alia* : George Alysbur(y).

Too the right | wyrschypffull | Master Botlar (?) at Swyneshe(d) | p. 233. a m d and xli and | xxxiii yere of his g | Rayne | The K. Jesses ffro | yourke to london h | warde.

A list of the stages follows, occupying nearly the length of the page.

p. 245. The names of Castels.   Two lists occupying most of the margin.

p. 279. List of Abbeys (23) mostly in Lincoln and Northants : Peterborwe, Croland, Spaldyng, etc.   Ending with Borne, Semperyngham, and Kyme.

Several times, by way of a joke, *loke apon the tother syde* has been written : there being either nothing to look at or some rude remark.

p. 331. List of bishoprics in England, Wales, and Ireland (Dublin and Meath only).

p. 330. List of counties in England.

p. 332, 3. List of dukes, marquises, earls, and barons.   There are 12 dukes, 2 marquises, 26 earls, and 51 barons.

p. 405. Nor god ama : | a Raffe Alesb. . . | . . . I pry | god and . . . | blesed lady.

p. 509. Martin Aylesbury swa ? | grome of the kechin | the xxij day of July h | xxxiii yere of hyes | Rayne and put to by Ca ? | denne.

p. 527. Martyn Aylesbury | owyth thes | booke.

On the fly-leaf is a note by Dr. Daniel Waterland :

Other Copies or Parts of Copies of this Book.

1. In the Library of Sylas Taylor gent. referrd to by Mr. Asmole in his *Order of the Garter*, p. 21, and by Mr. Hearn in his glossary to P. Langtoft's Chronicle.

2. Mr. Sheldon's copy referrd to by Mr. Hearn in the same Glossary.

SPECULUM HUMANAE SALVATIONIS, ETC.

C.M.A. 6765. 46, 6757. 38, 6762. 43.   [2359.]

Vellum, 12½ × 9, ff. 47 and 100.   Cent. xv, early.   Very well written.

Collation : 1⁸ (wants l. 2 : this quire inlaid) 2⁸–4⁸ 5¹⁰ (3 canc.) 6⁸ (wants 1, 8) 7⁸ | 8⁸–11⁸ 12⁶ 13⁸ 14⁶ 15⁸–17⁸ 18⁶ 19⁸ 20⁸ 21².

The writing of the two portions is very uniform, and so is the red flourishing of the blue initials.

I. Speculum Humanae Salvationis.

The recto of f. 1 is pasted over. It contained the end of the list of chapters from XXX onwards. The first six leaves have been damaged at the edges, and Pepys has mounted them very carefully.

The pictures (two at the head of each page) are careful pen and ink drawings. Very little colour has been applied; yellow for earth, blue for water, and red for blood sometimes occur.

Text begins:

Incipit speculum humane saluacionis
In quo patet casus hominis et modus reparacionis.

It ends with the Seven Joys of the Virgin:

Quod nobis omnibus prestare dignetur dominus ihesus christus
Qui cum patre et spiritu sancto est imperpetuum benedictus. Amen.

The pictures are as follows:

I.
   1. Fall of the Angels.
   2. Creation of Eve.
   3. Prohibition of the Tree.
   4. Temptation of Eve. The serpent a winged four-legged dragon with female head. The tree not represented.

II.
   5. Fall of Adam.
   6. Expulsion.
   7. Beginning of Toil.
   8. Noah's Ark. The dove with the olive branch.

III.
   9. The Angel and Joachim.
  10. The dream of King Astyages.
  11. The Spring shut up. (Cant.)
  12. Balaam and the Angel.

IV.
  13. Birth of the Virgin.
  14. Tree of Jesse.
  15. The Closed Gate.
  16. The Temple of Solomon.

V.
  17. Presentation of the Virgin.
  18. The golden table offered. Two men hold the (wooden) table. The sun in the sky.
  19. Jephthah's daughter sacrificed.
  20. The Queen of Persia in the hanging gardens.

VI.
  21. Marriage of the Virgin.
  22. Marriage of Tobias and Sara.
  23. The Tower Baris.
  24. The Tower of David.

VII.
  25. Annunciation.
  26. The Burning Bush.
  27. Gideon's fleece.
  28. Rebekah gives drink to Eliezer.

VIII.   29. Nativity.
        30. Dream of Pharaoh's butler. He lies with a heavy stone fastened by a short chain to his neck, and his feet in a small pair of stocks without visible division or fastening.
        31. Aaron's rod.
        32. The Sibyl and Octavian. She is seated in a chair with a desk across the arms of it.
IX.   33. Adoration of the Kings.
        34. The Magi adore the vision of the Child in the star.
        35. The mighty men bring water to David.
        36. The Queen of Sheba. Solomon on his throne (of enormous height, with twelve lions on the steps).
X.   37. Presentation of Christ.
        38. The Ark of the Covenant.
        39. The Golden Candlestick.
        40. Samuel offered in the tabernacle.
XI.   41. Flight into Egypt and Fall of Idols.
        42. The image of a Virgin made by the Egyptians as commanded by Jeremiah.
        43. The child Moses before Pharaoh puts a hot coal to his mouth.
        44. Nebuchadnezzar and the Image.
XII.   45. Baptism of Christ.
        46. The Brazen Laver.
        47. Naaman in Jordan.
        48. The Ark crossing Jordan.
XIII.   49. The three Temptations of Christ.
        50. Daniel destroys Bel and the Dragon.
        51. David overcomes Goliath.
        52. David kills the lion and bear.
XIV.   53. Mary Magdalene washes Christ's feet.
        54. Manasseh's penitence. He sits crowned: his legs in the stocks below the knee: the stocks have high posts through which his hands are passed, and a chain from each goes to a collar on his neck.
        55. The Prodigal Son returns.
        56. David and Nathan.
XV.   57. The Entry into Jerusalem. Jesus weeps.
        58. Jeremiah laments over Jerusalem.
        59. David's return with Goliath's head.
        60. Heliodorus chastised for his attempt to rob the Temple.
XVI.   61. The Last Supper.
        62. The Manna.
        63. The Passover.
        64. Melchizedek and Abraham.
XVII.   65. The soldiers fall back on seeing Christ.
        66. Samson overthrows Philistines.
        67. Shamgar kills 600.
        68. David kills 800.
XVIII.   69. The Betrayal.
        70. Joab kills Amasa.
        71. Saul and David.
        72. Cain and Abel (offering and murder).

XIX. 73. Christ mocked.
74. Hur suffocated by the spitting of the Jews.
75. Ham mocks Noah.
76. Samson blinded by the Philistines. He stands holding two pillars : four men take hold of his hair.
XX. 77. The Scourging.
78. Achior bound to a tree. (Judith.)
79. Lamech mocked by his wives.
80. Job mocked by the devil and by his wife.
XXI. 81. The crowning with thorns.
82. King Darius and his concubine Apemen, who takes off his crown. (1 Esdr.)
83. Shimei and David.
84. Hanun insults David's ambassadors.
XXII. 85. Bearing the Cross.
86. Isaac bears the wood.
87. The Heir killed by the wicked husbandmen.
88. The spies carry the bunch of grapes.
XXIII. 89. Christ nailed to the Cross.
90. Men smite on the anvil. Tubal Cain invents harmony from the sound. Jubal plays the harp.
91. Isaiah sawn in sunder from the shoulder.
92. The King of Moab offers up his first-born. (2 K. iii.)
XXIV. 93. The Crucifixion, with the Thieves and Mary and John.
94. Nebuchadnezzar's dream of the Tree.
95. Death of Codrus, King of Athens.
96. Death of Eleazar Maccabaeus.
XXV. 97. Christ on the Cross derided by the Jews, and His side pierced.
98. Michal mocks David.
99. Absalom pierced on the tree.
100. Evil-Merodach cuts his father's body to pieces.
XXVI. 101. The Virgin supports the body taken from the Cross.
102. Joseph's coat shown to Jacob.
103. Abel mourned by Adam and Eve.
104. Naomi refuses to be comforted.
XXVII. 105. The Entombment.
106. David at Abner's burial.
107. Joseph put into the pit.
108. Jonah cast into the sea.
XXVIII. 109. The infernal regions in four tiers. (*a*) Infernus purgandorum, in which is Christ. (*b*) Infernus puerorum non baptisatorum. (*c*) Infernus dampnatorum et diabolorum. (*d*) Devils.
110. The three children and angel in the furnace.
111. Daniel fed in the lion's den. (*Bel and Dr.*)
112. Cut out : it should be the ostrich freeing its young, shut up in a crystal case by Solomon, with the blood of the worm Schamir.
XXIX. 113. Cut out. Christ overcoming Satan.
114. Benaiah kills the lion.
115. Samson, astride the lion, rends it.
116. Ehud kills Eglon.
XXX. 117. The Virgin trampling on the Devil.
118. Judith slays Holofernes.

H

119. Jael slays Sisera.
120. Tomyris puts the head of Cyrus into a tub full of blood.
XXXI. 121. Christ leads the Fathers out of Hell.
122. The Exodus.
123. Abraham delivered from the fire.
124. Lot and his daughters delivered from Sodom. Lot's wife is a nearly full-length figure with joined hands, on a column.
XXXII. 125. The Resurrection.
126. Samson carries the gates. The wrong picture is given, of Samson about to pull down the columns.
127. Jonah cast up.
128. The stone which the builders rejected.
XXXIII. 129. The Ascension.
130. Jacob's ladder.
131. The lost sheep brought back by Christ.
132. Elijah taken up.
XXXIV. 133. Pentecost.
134. The Tower of Babel. Four men are working on it. Two at top with trowels. The one on *l.* says, *gylmer* (*gib mir*) *wazzer*. One below hands up a brick and says, *ny Rosy*. The one at top on *r.* says, *da mihi leterem*, and the man below hands up a bowl of water: by him also is a scroll, *da mihi laterem*.
135. The Giving of the Law. The Ten Commandments on scrolls. By mistake the artist has drawn instead of the children of Israel, the Virgin, Peter, Paul, John, and another, as in no. 133.
136. The miracle of the oil wrought by Elisha.
XXXV. 137. The Virgin surrounded by the places of Christ's birth and passion, viz. Nazareth, Bedleem, cenaculum in Ierusalem, ortus in quo captus est, domus Cayphe, pretorium pilati, locus caluarie, sepulcrum domini, mons oliveti. The subject is called: Conuersacio b. uirginis post passionem Christi.
138. Anna waits for the return of Tobias.
139. The woman looks for the lost piece of silver. The coins have crosses between four groups of three dots.
140. Michal given in marriage to another than David.
XXXVI. 141. Coronation of the Virgin.
142. David brings home the ark.
143. The woman clothed with the sun.
144. Solomon makes Bathsheba sit beside him.
XXXVII. 145. The Virgin intercedes for men. SS. Dominic and Francis on *r.*
146. Abigail meets David.
147. The woman of Tekoa and David.
148. The wise woman with Sheba's head.
XXXVIII. 149. The Virgin shelters mankind under her robe.
150. Tharbis defends the city Saba against Moses.
151. The woman at Thebez kills Abimelech.
152. Michal lets David escape.
XXXIX. 153. Christ shows his wounds to the Father.
154. Antipater shows his wounds to Julius Caesar.
(A leaf cut out, containing 155. The Virgin interceding with Christ.
156. Haman hung.)
XL. (157 gone. The Last Judgment.)

(158 gone. The Parable of the Talents.)
159. The Wise and Foolish Virgins.
160. The writing on the wall.
XLI. 161. The pains of Hell.
162. David's vengeance on his enemies.
163. Gideon and the men of Succoth.
164. Pharaoh and the Egyptians drowned.
XLII. 165. The bliss of heaven.
166. The Queen of Sheba and Solomon.
167. Picture gone: the upper part of the leaf cut off. The feast given by
Ahasuerus.
168. Picture gone: the upper part of the leaf cut off. Job's children
feasting.
XLIII. 169. Picture gone. Christ appears to a hermit and reveals to him the
Hours of the Passion.
170. Picture gone. Vespers. The Last Supper.
171. Compline. The Agony.
172. Matins. Christ before Caiaphas.
XLIV. 173. Prime. Christ before Herod.
174. Tierce. The Scourging and Mocking.
175. Sext. Pilate washing his hands. Christ bearing the Cross.
176. None. Crucifixion. Longinus' eye healed.
XLV. 177. Sorrows of the Virgin. A Dominican with nails in hand and feet
and a sword through his body.
178. The first sorrow. Presentation. Symeon's prophecy.
179. Second. Angel and Joseph. The Flight.
180. Third. Christ and the Doctors. The Virgin and Joseph (?) outside.
Joseph resembles Christ.
XLVI. 181. Fourth. The Betrayal.
182. Fifth. The Crucifixion.
(A leaf gone. 183. Sixth. The Entombment.
184. Seventh. The Virgin and the instruments of the Passion.)
XLVII. (185. The Seven Joys. The Virgin appears to a priest.)
(186. First Joy. Annunciation.)
187. Second. Visitation.
188. Third. Nativity.
XLVIII. 189. Fourth. Adoration of the Magi.
190. Fifth. Presentation.
191. Sixth. Christ and the Doctors.
192. Seventh. Coronation of the Virgin.

The verso, pasted over, was blank. It has the names of William Owen,
and of John, Henry, William, and Joseph Beaumont.

II. A collection of miracles of the Virgin: the hand is very similar to
that of the *Speculum*, and reminds me also of the script of the great
collection of miracles in the Sidney Sussex MS., no. 95.

There is no title.

Prologue. Quoniam mentes audiencium ad diuini amoris gaudia et ad
matris misericordie poscenda suffragia plus inuitant exempla quam docen-
cium uerba eiusdem sanctissime uirginis miracula que sparsum (-im) per

H 2

libros uidimus cunctis eciam (eam) uenerantibus in unum collecta exhibere
curauimus, etc.   I

—Ipsa igitur que mater est summe ueritatis cooperante gratia habitan-
tis in se spiritus sancti in mirabilium suorum presenti conscripsione a nota
mendacii nos exhibeat alienos.   Expl. prol.

Capitula of the three books.

1. De S. hildefonso tolenato (-tano) Archiep. cui b. v. celeste contulit indumentum.
                                                                    [Ward, 604
    Text. Fuit in Theoletano urbe quidam archiep. qui vocabatur Hildefonsus.

2. De clerico in mari demerso quem uirtus diuina per b. v. miro modo illesum ad
litus transposuit.   Fuit quidam clericus Stephanus nomine Gallus genere   640

3. Qualiter prefatus clericus a temptacione carnis est liberatus (postquam ieroso-
limam uenit).   *ibid.*

4. De quodam in mari merso quem sub aquis pallio suo contectum litus adusque
perduxit.   Duo b. d. gen. m. miracula narrare.   (This and cap. 5.)   626

5. De quodam abbate quem cum sociis a naufragio liberauit (in medio maris
britannici).   *ibid.*

6. De illo qui quadam mirabili territus visione ipsius seruicio totum se impendit.
Quoniam uigilacio sancta.   631

7. Qualiter hore seruicij eius institute fuerunt.   Consuetudo fidelium est.

8. De tunica matris domini omni thesauro preciosiore.   (A. d. 898. Rollo.)   603

9. De muliere que pre nimia inpunitate nasum ex toto perdiderat (in territorio
Carnotensi).

10. Qualiter dei genitrix cuidam apparens religioso se matrem esse dixit misericordie.
Quodam tempore dum beatus Oddo cluniacencis abbas.   603
    This chapter is marked in red in the margin as Cap. 1.   The first chapter of the
book has no such mark, but the others (2–9) are marked Capp. 2–9.

11. De columpnis, etc.   Columns at CPol raised by boys.   625

12. De abbate. ex libro Greg. Turon.   Abbot at Jerusalem : supply of corn.   642

13. Qualiter sedato scismate quod fuit inter Innocencium et Petrum Leonis Dominus
pacem reddiderit.   Teste apostolo didicimus.

14. De muliere cuius uultum sacer ignis occupauerat et.   In Galii uico qui dicitur
Dormiencium (A. d. 1103).

15. De mul. que alteri mul. uirum suum auferebat (in eodem uico).

16. De ymagine domini que cuidam infanti locuta est.   623

17. De sacrista quem a demonibus liberato (!) et ut penitenciam de reatibus ageret
ad uitam redire fecit.   In quodam monast. erat ymago

18. De alio sacrista quem sepeliri fecit in cuius lingua nomen v. aureis litteris
scriptum populus inuenit.   Commentariolum cuiusdam moderni continet.   cf. 632

19. De clerico qui ab ea carnis continenciam et gradum apostolicum obtinere meruit :
named Caesarius ; became pope Leo ; story of the hand cut off.   cf. 674

20. De Bonefacio ep. cui duodenos aureos reddidit quibus importunum nepotem suum
pacificauit (Greg. Dial.).

21. De monacho qui nomen eius diuersis scribebat coloribus quem in infirmitate
uisitauit et in regno dei collocauit.   Tranquillitatis amator monachus.

22. De milite cuius anima[m] cucullam ab ea accipere meruit quam habere dum
esset in corpore concupiuit.   Iustissimus vir b. Pachomius

23. De monast. quod terra in die resurreccionis absorbuit et anno transacto rediit
cum populo (apud Agliam).

24. De S. Dunstano Cant. arch. qui in Oratorio ipsius uoces psallencium audiuit.   631

25. De eodem uiro cui cum uirginibus occurrit et cum honore maximo ad oratorium eum perduxit. 632
26. De imp. CPolitano quem per annum in foueam posuit et ei angelos ad custodiendum deputauit. Imp. tercius CPolitane civitatis nomine Alexis. 675
27. De milite qui dixit quod non egebat ipsius auxilio qui statim cecidit fracto (collo).
28. De eo quem b. v. in uisione reda(r)guit: for not singing compline for her. Sid. Sussex, ii. 54 ?
29. De ymagine eiusd. v. que orante quodam institore Alexandrino locuta est multis audientibus. 638
30. Qualiter s. d. g. m. manum propriam restituit Iohanni Damasceno. 683

Inc. Lib. Secundus   f. 18^b

1. Qualiter b. v. apparuit S. Bonito Aluernarum ep. et ei celestem largita est uestem. Ex quo semel incepi, loquar adhuc de domina mea. 622
2. De clerico quem sepeliri fecit qui occisus extra cimiterium fuerat tumulatus (Chartres). 605
3. De quod. cler. quinquepartitum gaudium nunciante. 605
4. De paupere qui elemosinas sibi datas aliis pauperibus largiebatur. 605
5. De latrone quem uitam suspendio funere (!) non permisit b. v. m. (Abbo). Sicut exponit b. Greg. 606
6. De mon. quem sine confessione . . . defunctum a demonibus rapuit et ad uitam reuocauit. In monast. s. Petri ap. urbem Coloniam. 606
7. De illo qui a demonibus deceptas et a seipso interfectus per eam ad uitam rediit (Gerard at Cluny.). 606
8. De presb. illitterato. One mass. 607
9. De duobus fratribus quos a penis inferni misericorditer liberauit (Petrus & Stephanus). 607
10. De rustico male morigerato qui fraudem faciebat (removed landmarks: delivered by the Virgin). 607
11. De mon. quem eductum penali exitio in loco refrigerii collocauit. Prior at Pavia appears to Hucbertus. 608
12. Qualiter deuotum sibi clericum ad gradum pontificalem. . . . Jeronimus of Pavia. 608
13. De linceo tincto. Corporal of Clusa. 608
14. De ymag. b. v. quam ignis comburens reliquit. Mont St. Michel. 608
15. De cler. qui propter ipsius amorem . . . nupcias . . . postposuit. Canon of St. Cassian at Pisa. 609
16. De quad. mul. que per b. v. est sanata. Mulierdis (= Murieldis). 609
17. Qualiter b. v. quorundam militum presumpcionem digna cohercuit ulcione. 613
18. De monacha quam dei mater monuit ut angelicam salutacionem non cursum (-im) sed morose pronunciaret. Fertur fuisse ap. S. Edwardum Septonie (Shaftesbury). 614
19. Qualiter se deprecantis habundare fecit matrone fidelis insufficienciam. Mead multiplied. 614
20. De quodam languido cui b. m. pedem perditum restituit. (In urbe uiuaria.) 619
21. Quid ap. Toletum contigerit in festo assumpc. gl. v. matr. domini m. 610
22. De quodam . . . cui egrotanti mamillam suam, etc. (Rogerius). 613
23. De ymag. domini in virginis gremio residentis qui multis audientibus testimonium prebuit ueritati. Fuit quid. religiosus Leodiensis eccl. archidiac.
24. De quod. canonico cuius egrotantis linguam, etc. (Niucrnensis eccl. Decanus Teterius).
25. Item de prenominato dei seruo.

33. Qualiter d. g. quendam deuotum sibi famulum a demonibus ... liberauit (from Peter of Cluny). Fuit in ordine Cartusiensi.

Finis libri. Ecce que de b. d. g. Maria ex maiorum scriptis collegimus, etc.

—nobis placabilem reddat propicium d. n. I. C. qui cum p. et sp. s. uiuit et regnat deus per infin. sec. sec. Amen.

An examination of the various collections of Miracles described by Ward, *Cat. of Romances*, ii. 586 sqq., shows that this does not agree with any one of them with the exception of one large group (ii. 2–20). Hardly any of the Miracles seem to be unknown.

III. De exemplis patrum. 60b

Five stories from Vitae Patrum.

IV. Meditaciones et oraciones collecte ex dictis diuersorum sanctorum et aliis auctoritatibus. 62b

38 Capitula.

Prol. Oraciones siue meditaciones que subscripte sunt quoniam ad excitandum legentes, etc.

—propter quem facte sunt pietatis effectum.

1. Quod summa perfeccio humane uite est deo adherere per amorem. Cum enim mens amore et desiderio

38. Ends: te concupisco. Qui uiuis et regnas cum deo patre in unitate sp. s. deus. Amen.

V. Hic inc. capitula meditacionum S. Augustini ep. et doctoris de spiritu sancto. 95

23 Capitula.

Deus meus spiritus sancte timeo et desidero loqui tibi

Ends f. 100a—pullos suos pascat educat et perducat ad nidum illum eternum in quo cum deo patre et filio permanet in sec. sec. Amen.

f. 100b is pasted over. It has the capitula and beginning of the text of the Soliloquium of Augustine.

Vigili cura mente sollicita (*P. L.* xl. 847).

CATALOGUES OF MANUSCRIPTS. [2427.]

Paper, $12\frac{9}{10} \times 9$, ff. $28 + 154 + 11$. Cent. xvii. In a large clear hand. Red leather binding with gold tooling.

A device from an engraved title-page, cut out, is pasted upon the flyleaf.

Title : Bibliothecae Regia (in Palatio Sti Jacobi) et Cottoniana
Avec celle de S. A. R. le Duc d'Yorc.

1. Catalogus Librorum MSS. Bibliothecae Regiae in Palatio Sancti Iacobi. It is the catalogue which appears in Bernard's *Catalogi MSS. Angliae*, 1697, ii. 239.

2. Catalogus Bibliothecae Cottoniane, Anno 1674. Continet folia 86 (really 154). It is a classified Index to the manuscripts without references to the pages on which each tract begins. The following classification is prefixed.

Of Knights. { Garter.		186
Bath.		186
Golden Ffleece.		187
Of Turneam^ts & Duells.		219
Of particular persons of England.		
Of particuler Cittyes & Townes in England.		211
Of the Cinque Ports.		212
Of Marchandize & Monyes.		174
Abstracts out of Ancient Records.		165
Of Uniuersityes & Colledges.		213
Of the Holy Land.		213
Of Warr.		206
Miscellanies.		225
Bookes in Saxon Language.		241
Bookes in the Orientall Language.		245
An Alphabeticall Catalogue of the names of all the Authors and their Workes.		261
Romances.		219

This classification is not strictly followed in the text, which gives:

Libri Historici. — f. 2
„ Theologici. — 26
(Affairs of State) Italica, etc. — 46
More Theological Books beginning abruptly in f. 55
Libri Miscellanei. — 84
Scriptorum Nomina ordine Alphabetico. — 94^b
Ciuil & Canon Law. — 114^b
More Affairs of State. — 116
Of Monasteries, etc. — 117
Vitae Sanctorum. — 124^b
Libri Saxonici (1). — 130
Prophecyes. — 131
Of Law. — 132
Of Particular Townes in England. — 134
Cinque Ports. — 135
Uniuersities & Colleges. — 135^b
Holy Land. — 136
King of England Dominions in France. — 136
Tourneaments & Duells. — 136^b
Romanzes. — 137
Libri Saxonici (2). — 137
Libri orientales. — 140^b
(Letters and State Papers: Abstracts of Records.) — 141^b
(Of Parliaments.) — 150
(Acta Consilii.) — 152
(Merchandise, etc.) — 152-4

3. On smaller paper, ff. 11, in a large hand.
Catalogue des Livres au Cabinet de son Altesse Royale le Duc d'York.
Catalogued by sizes.
The manuscripts, etc., which occupy 2½ pages, are nearly all naval.

LIFE OF CHRIST. THE MIRROR. THE APOCALYPSE. THE PSALTER, ETC., IN ENGLISH.

C.M.A. 6754. 35.   [2498.]

Vellum, 13⅜ × 9¾, ff. 232, double columns of 52–54 lines. Cent. xiv, late. In a good clear hand.

Binding with Pepys' stamp: lettered: Wickleef's Sermons MS.

Collation: 1⁸ 2⁸ 3⁶ 4⁸–23⁸ 24 (three) 25⁸–30⁸ (wants 8).

On the fly-leaves are a note and a list of contents by Dr. Waterland.

Contents.

1. Life of Christ.

Of þe godhede of oure lorde suete Jhesu crist god almiʒth(i).   p. 1

Oure suete lord Jhesu crist vpe his godhede he was tofore all creatures

C. 2. Of þe concepcioun of swete Jhesu crist hou he was conceyued.

In þe tyme of þe kyng heroudes þat was paen and helde goddes folk in seruage and regned in jerusalem so was þere a goode man þat hiʒth zakari.

The last section is: hou Jhesus schowed hym twyes to his deciples.

Ending: And þe holy gost hem wissed and tauʒte and confermed her sarueoñ þorouʒ miracles þat jhesus dude for hem.

Here enden þe Gospels an hundreþ and sex · oute nomen þe passion of Jhesu crist. Do so þat god be þi frende.

It is in the main a translation of Gospels.

The right half of the last leaf is cut off: it was most likely blank. On p. 44 otherwise blank, in a hand of Cent. xvi (which, as will appear, is that of Stephen Batman) is:

> Brycrys gezet aramen
> Let reason rule the yᵗ this booke shall reede
> Miche good matter shalt thou finde in deede
> Thowghe some bee ill, doo not the reste dispize
> Consider of the tyme, else thow art not wize.

(This article is edited as *The Pepysian Gospel Harmony* by Miss M. Goates for the E.E.T.S., 1923.)

2. Mirror or glasse to Looke in (xvi).   p. 45

Many more þere ben þat han wil to heren rede Romaunce & geste...

þe prolouge endeþ now · lokeþ to þe merour etc....

Holy wrytt haþ a lykenesse unto a tre...

For lettre of holy wrytt is as it were a derke cloude

—þat alle goodes we mowen take wiþ hym þat is one in trinite.

The sermons begin on p. 50. Dom. 1 Aduent. Cum appropinquasset.

Jhesus com nere a cite þat is cleped Jerusalem

The last is :

In nathali unius confessoris sec. Math. Homo quidam peregre.
Hit was a man seide Jhesus Crist þᵗ went in pilgrymage
—so to deffenden his ʒift þat we moten comen to his blisse. Amen.
Of þe holy omelies now I wil blynne
God bringe vs to þᵗ blisse þere ioye is euer inne.

Cf. C.C.C. 282.

3. Here bigynnen good techinges of wise men wiþ þe ten hestes after-ward distinctelich expouned. 212
Salamon seiþ in alle þi werkes þenke on þe ende and þou schalt neuer don synne. Þenke þou schal dyʒe and þou nost whanne neuere
The exposition of the Decalogue begins p. 217.
Ends : his fader & his broþere and his spouse · god vs þider brynge for his grete merci. Amen.

Þe comaundementz expouned here enden I ʒou seie
Vnto þe blis of heuene god vs wisse þe weie.

5. Þapocalips on englissh : makeþ here gynnyng
After þis synful lyf: God graunt vs good wonyng. 226
Seint Poule seiþ þapostle þat alle þo þat willen priuelich leuen (Pro-logue of Gilbert).
—at oure begynnyng ʒif it be his wille. Amen.
Ich Johñ ʒoure broþer and pertynere in tribulaciouns and duelle in pacience.
—Philadelphe and Laodice.
(Gloss). By þe vndoyng. By seint Johñ ben bitokned þe good prelates of holy chirche þat vnderstonden þe voices of þe godspelles.
This is a translation of the French version edited by P. Meyer for the Soc. des Anc. Textes Français. (*L'Apocalypse en Français au XIII⁶ siècle*, 1901.)
Ends : in body and in soule . and duellen wiþ hym wiþouten ende. Amen.

Þe apocalips on Englissch : here now makeþ ende,
Vnto þe blis of heuen: god graunte vs grace to wende.

6. Of þe sautere on englisch: here is þe gynnynge
Wiþ þe latyn before: and Gregories expounynge.
The Latin is in red throughout. At the beginning is a pretty initial in outline with a dragon
Beatus vir—pestilencie et falsitatis non sedet. Blissed be þe man þat ne ʒede nouʒth in þe conseil of wycked . and ne stoode nouʒth in þe waie of synners · and ne satte nouʒth in fals iuggement.

The Latin includes very brief glosses which have been underlined in black.

The Psalter is followed by the *Cantica* ending with *Quicunque vult.*

—whiche bot if vche man it bileue stedfastlich and strongelich he ne may nouȝth be saued.

Ter quinquagenos cantat Dauid ordine psalmos
Versus bis mille, sex centum, sex canit ille.   p. 370

Col. 2 has notes by Stephen Batman.

ȝif euer thys booke don take his flight
on Stephan batman let it liȝhte
ȝit came to passe, and yt is trwe
I will not change it for no newe.

A learned pastor this book did make
and in those daies taken for great sapiens
The vewe dooth vrge a Christian to quake
the sight of souche blinde ignorance
Who wolde not but wayle souch a blindnes
that hathe benne the cause of muche wretchednes.

The first part is veri good
                thowghe a worde or two doo varie
The second is not sound
                smaule truthe dooth carie
Yet as the one wᵗoute the other thow cannot bee
Else falshod with trwthe mixed thow cannot see.

To answer the ennemy thow maiste be boulde
When theire owen penns such errowres have tolde.

Teare not this book . but kepe it in store
thow maiest else misse for knoweng of more.

The age of this book by conferring wᵗʰ an other coppy was written when k henry the . 4 . had busines agay(n)ste the welshmen anº 1401.

The Psalter is the same (as Miss A. C. Paues points out, *Engl. Studien*, xxx. 344) with that printed by Dr. Bülbring (E.E.T.S., *Earliest Complete Engl. Prose Psalter*) : a collation of this manuscript is to be given by Dr. Bülbring in the second part of his edition.

7. Heading by Batman : The Canticle vpon the Masse, with the kepyng, to discover (?) their wilfull blindnes and show (?) what straunge . . .   371

Rubr. Recti diligunt te.   In canticis canticorum . sponsa ad sponsum. Est rectum gramaticum . rectum geometricum, etc.

Lorde seiþ goddes spouse to her der worþe spouse . þe riȝth louen þe etc.

Hec est caritas illa quam describit apostolus . . .
—wiþ the innere reule þat reuleþ þe hert.
Now ich to deele þis booke on · viij distynctiouns.   373

Lib. II. Omni[a] custodia custodi cor tuum.

The divisions of the other parts are not clearly marked, but III begins on p. 387, col. 2 ; IV, p. 402, col. 2, sub fin. ; V, p. 425, col. 1 ; VI, p. 434, col. 2, sub fin. ; VII, p. 441, col. 2.

Ending 446, col. 1. Þis is þe riȝth loue þat reuleth þe hert wiþinnen þat euere owe to ben in worschipp ykept. Þis is þe seuenþe dele of þis booke.

Then follows a discourse on the vision of the New Jerusalem.

Now ichil tellen on of þe siȝttes þᵗ seint Johñ þe ewangelist seiþ
—bot ȝif he do as holy chirche biddeþ hym he ne may neuer come þere inne.

Now to men & wymmen þat ben bischette hij ne schullen ben yhouseled bot fiftene siþes in þe ȝere. 448
—no lesse hyre þan al hym seluen. Amen.

And ȝif it be ȝoure wille as ofte as ȝe it reden 449
—wille haue mercy on hem for his dere moder loue. Amen.

Þis goode booke Recluse : here now makeþ ende
Vnto þe blis of heuen : god graunte vs grace to wende.

The above is an abridged version of the *Regula anachoritarum* attributed to Simon de Gandavo, Bishop of Salisbury (d. 1315), but really by some earlier author. The older version was edited for the Camden Society in 1853 by the Rev. J. Morton. The present version diverges from the original particularly in the last section, which very imperfectly represents Part VIII of the original. The section on the New Jerusalem does not occur there.

Miss A. C. Paues has written on this manuscript (l. c.) and given short extracts.

8. Of oure lefdy marie : bigynneþ now here þe pleynt
Þᵗ of þe passion of hir son sche telde wᵗ herte feynt. 449
Oure swete lefdy seint marie goddes moder of heuene after þe stiȝinge vp of hir swete son Jhesu crist vpon þe fyftenþe day of August lyued here fiftene ȝere.

She narrates the Passion, in the first person. There are some Northern forms, " tellande and prechande."
—þe joye that ich hadde whan I seiȝe my swete son arisen passed alle þe ioyes þt euere ich hadde fro þe tyme þat I was borne, ȝe þat haue herd þis tale þe blissinge of my swete son J. C. mote ȝe haue & myne. And alle also þat it writen etc. . . . in my son regne wiþ þe fader & þe son & þe holy gost þat lyueþ and regneþ wiþ outen ende. Amen.

Þe passione as oure lefdy seiþ : of Ihesu endeþ here
In to þe blisse of heuen : vs bringe it all in fere.

9. Nicodemus Gospel (xvi).   459

þe gode man & þe noble prince Nichodemus þat priuelich was Jhesus deciple ... I schal telle ȝou a smal book þᵗ he made of þe passioun & of his vp arisyng.   Þᵗ fel on þat ilche day þat he aros.   Þe bischopes & þe princes

—and for alle þe soules þat goddys mercy abiden seiþ a pater noster & an Aue Maria.

Of þe vprist of Crist : as Nichodemus gan telle
Here now make ich ende : god schilde vs alle from helle.

It is a version of the last part of the *Gesta Pilati*, from cap. xii (Tischendorf, p. 367) onwards.

See Hulme, *Harrowing of Hell*, E.E.T.S., Extra Series, p. xxxiv.

10. Five prayers in English.   463

(*a*) Swete fader of heuene
(*b*) Swete lorde Jhesu crist goddes son
(*c*) Swete lorde I. C. fader & son & holy gost
(*d*) Lefdi seint Marie als wis as þou art moder
(*e*) Alle halewen I biseche ȝou

Batman has written a certain number of remarks in the volume.

CHRONICLES, CORONATIONS, ETC.

C.M.A. 6718. 3.   [2516.]

Paper, 14 × 9⅘, ff. 4 + 124, 46 lines to a full page.   Cent. xvi.   In neat Gothic hand.

Old binding, rough skin over boards ; four flat pieces of metal on each cover, four-petalled, engraved with fleurs-de-lys in circles on the petals and with a small boss in the centre of each : metal clasp.   Rebacked, lettered Ceremon. Curiae Angl. MSS.   Pepys' stamp in gold on the sides.

Collation : a⁴ 1¹⁸ 2¹⁶–4¹⁶ 5⁶ 6²⁰ 7¹² 8⁸ 9¹².   The first and last leaves line the covers.

On 18ᵃ is a letter

To yᵉ Ryht Worᵘˡˡ Edward Cooke Esq. Attorny Generall to her Maᵗʸᵉ. from D. Hille Esq. (?) dated at Lincoln 21 Aug. 1597, presenting this book, given to the writer by a " speciall frynd, an auncient observer of antiquities."

Affixed are these lines :

Heu poterim dando daniell exponere amorem?
Ast poterit Nomen danihill [i.e. da nihil] esse meum

If þowe as wyll coulde daniels Love make knowne
Then Daniell styll but now da nill alone.

In the cover in an older hand is : Gulielmi Suerderi.

On 10^b : a partial Index.

On f. 1 at top : Edw. Coke.

Contents. The first section contains brief chronicles of the world and of England in particular.

De creacione mundi.   1

De regnis et ciuitatibus maioribus et de Bretonia.   1^b

De dilatacione fidei christiane et Ortum Relegionum.   2^b

De ortu Relegionum.   3

De quibusdam personis famosis et de preliis (St. Alban to the plague of 1377).   3^b

Etates mundi 5.   Verba Bruti, Responcio Diane   5^b

Hic inc. Cronica bona et compendiosa de Regibus Anglie tantum a Noe usque in hunc diem.   5^b

Noe fuerunt tres filii

Ends with Henry IV.   Idem henricus magis mirabilius vitam miserabiliter terminauit.

Also in C.C.C. 21. 4, 177. 38 (to Richard II).

Section 2 relates to Coronations.

Processus factus ad coronacionem Regis Ricardi secundi, etc.   12^b

    Decedente de nutu summi preceptoris

First : seruicia dominorum ad coronacionem.

    Officiarii principales Regis in die Coron.   17^b

    Auctoritas Senescalli anglie 19 Marescalli 20

Ces sont les usages que Thomas de Brotherton ffitz au Roy clamoit, etc. in French.   20

Coronacio.   Die vero S. Swithuni   23

Oraciones dicende super Regem et Reginam.   24^b

Le o(r)dre pur faire lez chiualer de la Bathe.   27

The obseruant of the ordre how the kyng of England shall behaue hym selfe in hys Coronacion & the ordre of the quene, etc.   29

Modus tenendi parliamentum.   Hic discribatur modus, etc.   32

    With some marginalia of various dates.

Modus faciendi duellum coram Rege, in French.   35^b

Thorder of the kyngys howse of Englande w^t thofficers of ye same, in French.   38^b

Ceste le ordenauns a enoindre et Coroner le Roy de ffraunce.   56^b

    With the office in Latin.   Followed by Benedictio vexilli, with Litany, 65^b.   Serement dez pers de ffraunce, 66.   And oaths of other officials.

List of Saints buried at St. Denis.   67^b

List of Kings.   Dagobert to Charles V.

Principal Relics.   69
    69^b–72^b blank.
The Coronation of Kyng Henry the viij^{te}.   73
    Here foloweth a device for the maner & ordre, etc.
    —And also the moost noble & excellent princesse dame Katerine daughter of (blank), etc.
    86^b, 87 blank.
    Supplementary directions. ffor as moche as theire ys nowe but lytell knowlege of the Syttyng in Estate of the Dukes, etc.   88
    An unfinished copy going as far as the directions for the Day of Estate in the Hall.
A second copy in another hand.   93
    Including directions for the queen, for the creation of a prince, marriage of a prince's daughter, etc., the last unfinished.
    As for making of the knyghtes of the bathe, 113. As for the College of Wyndesore ffor Seynt Georges fest, 113.
    De apparatu principis qui migrauit de hoc seculo. Partly in Latin. 114
    As for beriyng of a prince nye of the blode Ryall.   114^b
    The beryeng as for an erle.   115^b
    The enterment of the erle of Saresbury at Bresham in the shire of Buk. (15 Feb. 2 Ed. IV).
    The last article (without title) is a letter.   117^b

To sey to you at what tyme the quene w^t chylde shall take hir chamber and what persones shall do hir seruyce that is in acte and so is ye purificacioun to and there in cañ margarete stanlow me bromeley enforme yow best of any that I knowe, etc. The writer answers various points, referring to the usage of Henry IV and V and ends: Sir one thyng I used alwey and so I wolde councell yow yf my lorde chambreleyn were present. I did never no grete thyng in myn office but by his aduyce which was to me sufficient warrant. The boke whiche all these be in acte in was wont to be alwey in the housholde the last man that I understande that had it was hampton the esquyer.

On a fly-leaf at the end is a later note of Incidents of Inheritaunce.

WYCLIFFITE SERMONS, ETC.

C. M. A. 6753. 34.   **[2616.]**

Vellum, 14 × 9½, ff. 2 + 109, double columns of 55 lines. Cent. xiv, late. In a good, clear hand: brown ink. Some ornament of good English style rather rough in execution.

Collation: 2 fly-leaves, one lining the cover. 1⁶ 2¹²–6¹² 7⁶ (+ 4 (4 canc.) after 4) 8¹² 9¹² 10⁸ 11² (2 lining cover).

The second fly-leaf is from an account roll of Edward III's time, a good deal obscured by the bookplate, headed :

Medium tempus
Die mercurii primo die Augusti
De Priore s. trinitatis Norwic. coll. x° bienn. R. a clero a° xx° conc.   Dioc. Norwic.
x. li. de primo termino secundi anni eiusdem x°.
De ffratre Hugone Michel Precept.
De Abbate de Derleye coll. x°.
De Abbate b. marie Ebor.
De Priore de Tutebury Alien.
De Abb. Glouc.
De Abb. de Pippewell.
De Herueo ffastolff persona ecclesie . . .
De Priore S. trinitatis N . . .
De Vic' Albredo de Witlesbury.
De Will° de humberston mercatore . . .
De Joh. de Outhorp mercatore de lincoln c⁴ de mutuo.
De Abb. Glaston.   etc.

1. Wyclif's Homilies on the Ferial Gospels.   p. 1
Hic inc. Euangelia fferialia.   fferia quarta dominice prime a⟨d⟩uentus domini.   Principium euangelii.
As men schulden trowe in crist
Edited by T. Arnold, *Select English Works of J. Wyclif*, vol. II, p. 1 (Oxford, 1871).
The page is bordered.   The ornament recalls that in a Trinity Hall MS. no. 17.
Ending p. 158 : as Poule speketh (Arnold, p. 217).
Expl. euang. ferialia tocius amni (*sic*).

2. Homilies on the Proprium Sanctorum (Arnold, vol. i, p. 295).   109
In vigilia S. Andree.
This gospel telleþ in storye hou crist gederede his dysciples
This page is bordered.
The Sermon for All Saints ends p. 158: to telle goddes lawe & hys wylle (Arnold, i. 412).

3. Then follows Exposicio euangelii Math. 24.
Egressus Jhesus de templo . . . Þis gospel telleþ muche wisdom (Arnold, ii. 393, *Of Mynystris in þe Chirche*).
Ending p. 174 : but not raueyschen þere hope in crist.

4. Hic inc. Comune Sanctorum.   174
Ego sum vitis vera.   As comyn þing is better (Arnold, i. 165).
Ending p. 215 : in whuche þey schulen be deede (l. c. p. 294).
Expl. Comune Sanctorum.

I

On p. 217 are these verses written twice in a hand of cent. xv:

> Munus est iudex fraus est mercator in orbe
> Nec lex est dominis nec timor ⟨est⟩ pueris
> Ingenium dolus est amor hominis (omnis?) ceca voluptas
> Ludus rusticitas et gula festa dies
> Etas ridetur mulier pulsatur amore
> Diues laudatur pauper ⟨et⟩ heret humo
> Prudentes ceci cognati degeneres sunt
> Mortuus ignotus nullus amicus amat.

Also, later: God spede truth.

At the beginning (f. ii^a) are some notes by Dr. Waterland, identifying the writer as Wyclif and referring to two other manuscripts at St. John's (C. 8) and the University Library 345 (= li. 1. 40).

He also gives a list of references to anti-papal passages.

ISIDORI ETYMOLOGIAE.

C.M.A. vac.   [2808.]

Vellum, $15\frac{1}{2} \times 10\frac{3}{4}$, ff. 131, double columns of 50 lines. Cent. xii, late. Finely written in an upright hand. fo. 2 Et valeas. *or* cia dialetica.

Collation: $1^8–7^8\ 8^{?8}$ (wants 3? replaced by two paper leaves : also 8) 9^4 (2 replaced by 2 paper leaves) $10^8–14^8$ (wants 3–6 replaced by 4 paper leaves) $15^8\ 16^8\ 17^6$. I reckon the paper leaves in the foliation.

A good many edges of leaves have been cut off in the latter part of the book.

Isidori Etymologiae.
 Ysidori epistola ad Braulionem.   I.
  Domino meo et dei seruo
   —ora pro nobis beatissime domine.
 Item epistola Braulionis ad Ysidorum.   I
  Domino meo et vere domino
   —illustrari mereamus.
 Et (Ut) valeas que requiris cito in hoc corpore inuenire. 2
  —instrumentis equorum.
 Domino meo . . . braulioni—domine et frater.   2
 Domino meo . . . ysidoro braulio—non marcescens.
 Isidore to Braulio. Domino meo . . . Tue sanctitatis epistole 2^b
 Item.   En tibi sicut pollicitus sum   2^b
 Inc. capitula gramatice artis ysidori (35)   2^b
 Inc. lib. primus ethimologiarum S. Ysidori archiep. hyspalensis. de disciplina et arte.   2^b
  Disciplina a discendo

Lib. II, 12ᵇ; III, 20; IV, 27ᵇ; ‚V, 30ᵇ, VI, 37; VII, 43ᵇ, VIII, 57ᵇ; IX, 58 (lacuna in capp. 2–4).
Two full-page diagrams of affinity on p. 65. The first has very rough heads.

X, 65ᵇ (lacuna A–P); XI, 69; XII, 74; XIII, 82; XIV, 86ᵇ, XV, 93; XVI, 99 (lacuna in capp. 15–26 and XVII 1–5 part); XVII, 108; XVIII, 114; XIX, 118ᵇ; XX, 125ᵇ. On 129ᵇ a circular mappa mundi, a labyrinth, and a circular diagram of the mountains in Thessaly.

Text ends 129ᵃ: ignis ardore siccatur. Expl. lib. ethimol. b. ysidori hispaliensis archiep.

On 130 in the same hand:

Inc. Epistola Iohannis regis indie ad emanuelem constantinopolitanum imperatorem.

Presbiter iohannes potentia et uirtute dei et d. n. I. C. Rex regum terrenorum (Ed. by Zarncke)

Ending 131ᵇ:

Que si uales cum ceterorum regum diuiciis compara. valete.

The writing of this book is very good: the ornament rough and provincial. It is almost confined to decorative initials in bright colours: no gold is used.

FRAGMENTS OF MANUSCRIPTS.
C.M.A. vac. [2981.]

Large folio: paper, with some fragments of manuscripts pasted on both sides of the leaves, and descriptions written in large fair hand about them. Only those fragments which are of mediaeval date will be noticed here: there are some specimens of early printing as well.

The greater part of the collection consists of copy-books of the sixteenth and seventeenth centuries, taken to pieces, and the leaves, engraved on one side only, pasted in, several on a page.

Title: My Calligraphical Collection, vol. I.

Comprehending as well Original Proofs of the Hand-writings of the Ancients in Several Ages within the last 1000 Years; and the Competition for Mastery between Librarians and Printers, upon the first breaking-out of the Latter
as the Performances of all the Celebrated Masters of the Penn (now Extant and Recoverable) whether Domestick or Forreign, by Hand or Burin, within the last and praesent Age.
Put together Anno Domini 1700.

Followed by elaborate tables of contents filling four leaves.

Second title-page :

Original Proofs of Antient Hand-Writing, English & Foreign, between the years 700 & 1500.

Third title-page :

Proofs of Antient Hand-Writing, with the Opinion of that Eminent Critick in re Diplomaticâ, our Country-Man Mr. Humphrey Wanley of Oxford, touching the different Ages, Characters, & Countrys of yᵉ ſd Pieces, in Return to my Enquiries from him on that behalf.

The specimens have only the one side exposed, except in the case of nos. 18, 19, which is regrettable.

No. 1. Vellum, 4⅖ × 6½, 17 lines, sloping minuscule with uncial forms (N̄), and rubrics in uncial. Cent. viii ?

From Isidore Etymol. III. xli–xlii. 4.

III. *De gemina facie caeli.* Facies caeli uel caput orientalis |

Ends : quorū primū ē meroiſ secundū ſenoiſ (Syene).

Wanley (whose notes will not be given in full) says : ' Written in France about the time of Charles the Great, but rather before than after.' He compares with Bede on the Canonical Epistles in the Bodleian Library, written 818. ' This (the fragment) appears more ancient.'

Refers to the last specimen on p. 361 of Mabillon *de Re Diplom.*

No. 2, p. 2. A whole leaf of a Gospel book. Cent. viii.

12³⁄₁₀ × 8½, 20 lines, in a magnificent Anglian round hand. Initials filled with brown-red, green, and yellow, and encircled with red dot . Eusebian Canons marked in the margin.

Wanley : Written in England, middle or end of the 8th century.

The text of the exposed side is Luke x. 39–xi. 5 *a.*

Erat soror· nomine maria ꝗ etiam sedens | secus pedes dn̄i audiebat uerbum illius· M|artha ħ (autem) satagebat circa frequens ministe| rium q: stetit Et ait dn̄e non est tibi cura quod | soror mea reliquit me solaministrare· Dic | ergo illi ut me adiuuet· Et respondens dixit illi | ih̄s martha martha sollicita es· Et turbaris | circa plurima porro unum est necessariū | maria optimam partem elegit q; non aufere|tur ab ea : Et factum est cum esset in loco | quodam orans ut cessauit dixit unus ex disci|pulis eius ad eum· Dn̄e doce nos orare· Sicut | Et Iohannes docuit discipulos suos· Et ait illis | cum oratis dicite, Pater noster sc̄ificetur | nomen tuum ; adueniat regnum tuum ; Fiat uolun|tas tua : sicut in caelo Et in terra ; panem n̄m co|tidianum da nobis hodie Et dimitte nobis pec|cata nostra, siquidem et ipsi dimittimus omni | debenti nobis ; Et ne nos inducas in temptatio|nem :· :· Et ait ad illos quis uestrum habet

Some of the punctuation is added. Of the abbreviation marks over the n̄m the upper one is certainly red.

It is a first-class specimen. Possibly the book it belongs to may be still extant, but I cannot so far identify it.

No. 3. From a Psalter.

$3\frac{1}{2} \times 5\frac{4}{5}$, 6 lines, fine large upright insular hand.

Wanley: Fragments of the 38th (37th) Psalm, written in England, perhaps about the end of the 8th century.

Inimici autem mei uiuent | et confor-tati sunt su|per me· Et multi-plicati s̄t | qui me hoderunt iniqui· | Qui retribuebant mihi | mala pro bonis . de tra . (xxxvii. 20, 21*a*).

There are a few interlinear glosses of cent. xii–xiii?

No. 4. p. 3 from Dan. viii, 3–7*a*.

$7\frac{7}{10} \times 5\frac{1}{10}$, 20 lines, excellent Anglo-Saxon hand, same type as no. 2 but not so fine. Initials surrounded with dots.

Wanley : Written also in England : he compares the Durham Liber Vitae—the portion written in or before Egbert's time, whose death he puts in 836.

meos et uidi· Et ecce aries unus stabat ante paludé.

The page ends: Efferatus est | in eum· Et percussit arietē· Et commi|

No. 5. Scholia on Martianus Capella.

$10\frac{1}{10} \times 7$, 32 lines, fine English hand. Cent. ix.

Wanley: About the time (as I guess) of K. Alfred.

Begins: Nc̄ g⁰ (nunc ergo) .i. locuntʳ et dicunt. ītminatas ēē miytos .i. finitas | fabulas.

— latoia chelis .i. appollinis lira ;

DE GRAMMATICA

Rursum .i. iterato parat. camena .i. satira ł (uel) musa
— titulus hic p*ro* fine ponit*ur*. Et uenit.

No. 6, p. 6. A leaf. Scholia on Sedulius Carm. I. 310–316.

7×4, 24 lines, fine round upright minuscule. Cent. x ? North French.

Wanley: I doubt whether this was written by an English hand. End of the 10th or beginning of the 11th century.

Heretici inter se . Producere . aduenire . sectas .i. erores uel contentiones. Exerta .i. extensa uel nudata Retecto uidel. pallio Nil docti .s. sunt .i. nil scientes . . . Hic loquitur .i. arrius. Ille tacet .i. sabellius Hic ambulat .i. arrius inter .ɪɪɪ.ᵉˢ p*er*sonas : hic stat .i. sabellius. cu*m* una *p*ersona. Alter amat fletus .i. arrius . . . Alter cr̃ipsare cachinnu*m*, etc.

— Ridebat eni*m* q*ui*a uidebat homines huius s*ecu*li turpia lucra sectari.

No. 7. A leaf of Priscian.

$6\frac{4}{5} \times 4\frac{4}{5}$, 37 lines. Cent. xi. Fine hand : very minute marginal and interlinear notes.

Wanley: Written here in England not much after No. 6.

Poss*unt* uel num*er*i . ut tullii . ager agri . agro agru*m*
— ut uirg*i*l . in .*ii*. aenei*d* . hoc erat alma.

No. 8. A leaf of a service-book.

$7\frac{1}{10} \times 4\frac{3}{5}$, music, four-line stave in red (the top has five lines), and 10 of text. Cent. xii late? (so Wanley).

? From a manuscript now in Bp. Cosin's Library at Durham. (V. v. 6.) Begins in a hymn for St. Eadburga of Winchester.

Sanat paraliticum deum exorando Diuersorum generum morbis laborantes Virgo reddit alacres christum collaudantes Tali flore ditata letare wintonia De cuius transitu gaudet celi curia. In hac ergo die festa nobis iesu bone presta per Edburge merita vt nos saluet a peccatis et in regno claritatis collocet per secula amen.

In Octa$\bar{\text{v}}$ Pas$\bar{\text{c}}$.

Laudes saluatori uoce modulemur supplici Alleluia
Et deuotis melodiis celesti domino iubilemus messie
Qui seipsum exinaniuit ut nos perditos liberaret
homines Carne gloriam deitatis oculens.

No. 9, p. 7. Part of leaf.

$7\frac{2}{5} \times 5$, 14 lines, large round upright Italian hand. Cent. xii. Wanley: This I fancy might be written in Italy about the same time . . . with no. 8, 'looks like a fragment of some commentary upon Colossians i. 16.'

Ut ipsa officiorum uocabula exsequamur Uirtutes et enim uocantur illi nimirum spiritus per quos signa et miracula frequentius fiunt.

Principatus etiam uocantur qui ipsis quoque bonis angelorum spiritibus presunt qui subiectis a

No. 10. A deed. 7 Edw. III.

$4 \times 3\frac{4}{5}$, 10 lines.

Roger ffouke rector ecclesie de Shipton dedi . . . Roberti le Mir' de Blechesdñ . . . duo cotagia in Blechesd*en* etc. (Blechingdon, Oxon.).

Test: Tho. de Mosegraue Jo. de Croxford Jo. clerico de Blechesd*em* Will⁰ Rolf de eadem Jo. de Goseuord de eadem Rob. atte Buyte. Dat. ap. Blechesd*en* in fest. S. Mich. Arch. A. r. R. Edw. tercii post conquestum septimo.

No. 11. A leaf of a law book.

$7 \times 4\frac{1}{2}$, 31 lines, neat sloping hand. Cent. xv. 3rd and 4th chapters of a statute: headline 'quarto'. At bottom in large letters: Wyggemore.

No. 12 *a, b*. Two leaves of a Kalendar.

$5\frac{4}{5} \times 3\frac{4}{5}$. Well written. Cent. xiv late?

Months of January and March, Sarum Kalendar with Cisio Janus at the foot.

Wolstan (Jan.) in red ; also Cuthbert (Mar.).

Probably from an astronomical book. There are five columns of tables preceding the entries.

Gradus signorum.

No. 13. A leaf of a Psalter.

$4\frac{9}{10} \times 3\frac{1}{2}$, double columns of 32 lines. Cent. xv.

    Notus in iudea & Voce mea ad dominum (part).

No. 14. A leaf cropped.

$5 \times 3\frac{1}{10}$, 20 lines. French hand of cent. xv, getting toward lettre bâtarde.

From a Litany of Saints, quite undistinctive.

Wanley takes the line fillings for ragged staves and inclines to connect them with Beauchamp, Earl of Warwick, but is mistaken.

No. 15. A leaf.

$6\frac{7}{10} \times 4\frac{4}{5}$, 33 lines. A pretty law hand of cent. xv, first half: capp. I–III of the Statute of 1 Henry VI.

A very pretty flourished border (3 sides) and initial.

No. 16, p. 9. Fragment.

$5\frac{3}{10} \times 6\frac{1}{2}$, 15 lines. Fine large round hand. Cent. xi early ?

Wanley: a fragment of Ælfric, Abp. of Canterbury, his Homily De fide Catholica.

See the Ælfric Society's edition, by Thorpe, 1843, vol. i, p. 284, lines 6–22 : þæt þæt lator bið—Is hwæðere se sunu ana geflæscha⟨mod⟩ There are no important variants.

No. 17. A leaf from a Mathematical treatise.

$7\frac{7}{10} \times 5\frac{4}{5}$, broad left margin with diagrams, 25 lines of text. Good pointed hand. Cent. xiii.

Figure numerorum sicut 1. 2. 3. ꝝ ꝙ. 6· ᴧ. 8. 9 et cet. prima unitatis.

No. 18. Slip in uncials.

$1\frac{1}{2} \times 8$, 2 cols., 4 lines in each. Uncials.

Wanley : This is a Fragment of the Gospell of St. Matthew taken from a MS. copy of the gospells in the Cathedrall Library at Durham. As to the Hand; It is English, & bears a good Resemblance to a Latin Charter of Hlotarius King of Kent now extant in the Cotton Library (Augustus II), which bears date indictione septima, i. e. about the year of our Lord 679. For this reason, I guess the said Book . . . to be at least a thousand years old.

No. 19. A similar slip.

$1\frac{1}{5} \times 7\frac{9}{10}$, 3 lines, in a splendid Anglian half uncial.
Wanley: This is a Fragment of a Prologue praefixt to St. Luke's
Gospell, taken from a MS. copy of the Gospels in the same Library . . .
at least as old as . . . Nero D. iv (the Lindisfarne Gospels).

Memdum—That these 2 were a Present to me, from my most hon^d
& reverend Friends, the Dean & Chapter of Durham, An^o Dom^{ni}
1700.

A letter from Mr. C. H. Turner, of Magdalen College, Oxford (Feb. 19,
1909), points out that no. 18 comes from the Durham MS. A. II. 16, and
no. 19 from A. II. 17.

The text of no. 18 is:

recto (should be verso)

Matt. xii. 15, 16.		xii. 23^b, 24.	Dauid
inde et secuti sunt eum		numquid hic est filius	
multi et curauit eos	? cxxi		
omnes et praecipit eis	11 mℭxxi	Pharissei autem audien	
ne manifestum eum	(*red*) mɼxxxii	tes dixerunt hic non iecit	
	lū cxxuij		
		demones nisi in belzebud	

verso (should be recto) xi. 29, 30.	xii. 7, 8.
et humilis corde et inue	quid est uolo misericordiam
nietis requiem animab;	et non sacrificium numquam
uestris iugum enim	condempnasetis inno
meum suaue est et ho	centes dns est enim filius

Mr. Turner calls the hand more or less Italian. The Canons are in an
insular hand.

No. 19 text. From Prologue to Luke: recto and verso should be
transposed.

recto:

missa est ut requirentib; demonstraret in quo | ad praehendens erat (per)
                                                                  generationis
nathan filium (david) introitu | recurrentis in dm congregationis admisso
indis

verso:

secutus usq. ad confessionem eius seruiens dño | sine crimine nam neq.
uxorem umquam habe|ns neq. filios septuaginta quattuor annorum

p. 11. An Extract out of the preface . . . of . . . Major Ayres before
his Copy Book of the year 1698.

p. 12 and following have many specimens pasted on them, manuscript and printed, not separately numbered.

p. 12. *a.* Part of a leaf of a Manual with the Burial Office. Cent. xiii. Fine large upright hand; foreign.

b. 3½ × 5¾, five lines in a very large fine hand, from a Pontifical. English, cent. xiii.

serenos · Inde etiam moy|si famulo tuo manda|tum dedisti. Ut aaron fratrem | suum prius aqua lotum | per infusionem huius unguen|

c. Part of leaf of a thirteenth-century Bible in small fine hand : double columns. Parts of Apoc. xx–xxi.

d. A leaf of the same late Horae as no. 14, with the Psalm Quemadmodum desiderat.

e. Part of a leaf in double columns. Cent. xiii–xiv. A canon law book.

p. 13. *a.* Part of a leaf from the same MS. as no. 14. Hours of the Holy Sacrament or Corpus Christi.

b. Part of a leaf, 12 lines. xiii.
From a book of Exempla?
inquit fecisti michi . quia musce quas amouisti iam plene erant sanguine . et parcius molestabant me . que autem superuenient recenter acrius pungent me. Sic et procuratores uel officiales recenter substituti acrius in subiectos deseuiunt [rubric illegible to me]. Cum autem quadam die more solito incitaret aggrippa tyberium ut extraheretur auriga suus de carcere. Respondit ad ipsum ei non expedire cum in presentia ipsius uellet eum vinculatus accusare. Et cum in nullo sibi conscius esset aggrippa testatus est se uelle ut extraheretur et accusaret.

c. Part of a leaf of a thirteenth-century Bible in very small hand ; double columns. A fragment of Judith.

p. 14. Fragment of a leaf of a very large Spanish choir book (cent. xv or xvi) with music on 5-line stave.

p. 15. *a.* A leaf, 6 lines of text and six of music (neums? not on a stave). Cent. xii? Foreign.
Domine exaudi . . . et clama. Ne auertas.

b. Part of a leaf. Service book in double columns, fine hand. Cent. xii. English. Lessons. v (part) and vi from Maccabees : vii Ydropis morbus fratres ab aquoso humore : viii Ydropicus fratres comparatur diuiti auaro.

c. A slip, 8 lines of text and neums. Cent. x?
Part of office of a Virgin with Antiphons.
Diffusa est. Adducentur. Offerentur regi. *Euan* Simile est regnum.

Secreta Presta ques. dñe dš ñr ut sicut in tuo conspectu mors est pretiosa sanctorum ita eorum mentes uenerantium accepta tibi reddatur oblatio ꝑ
Simile est regnum
References to S. Prisca, S. Agatha, Octab. S. Agnetis.

d. Most of a leaf. Service book, cent. xiv. Music on 4-line stave. Foreign. A rubric *virg. xi. mill.*

e. A leaf from the same MS. as no. 8. Sequences for (1) S. Stephen (end). Tu et nobis martir o Stephane sempiterna impetra gaudia. (2) S. John. Johannes iesu christo multum dilecte uirgo.

pp. 16, 17. Text only. p. 18 blank.

p. 19. An original Copy-Book of about the year 1400 in use among the Librarii or Book-Writers before the coming-in of Printing.

The last page of the book is pasted on to the sheet. In consists of 5 leaves, vellum, stitched together. $5\frac{3}{10} \times 4$. Cent. xv early.

p. 1. Very large monogram Ihc in pale brown. A green cross-beam runs through the top of the *h* and is pierced with two nails, the bottom of the shaft of the *h* is pierced with one nail. All the monogram is pierced above by a green spear, below by the reed and sponge.

Below, 4 lines of text headed by a red cross.

The Alphabet ending z $\div$ est amen. Two forms of *a, r, s.* Then the alphabet a–z written as one word. Then honorificabilitudi.

p. 2. Alphabet a–z $\div$ est. Two forms of *a, r, s.* As on p. 1, but larger.

Confitemini domino quoniam bonus · quoniam in seculum misericordia eius.

p. 3. Alphabet in Gothic capitals. Two forms for each letter (3 for s): goes down to V.

pp. 4–7. Alphabet in blue capitals with red flourishing and also (between the larger letters) in smaller red capitals, plain.

p. 8. A beginning of a more elaborately flourished alphabet in outline only. A, B, C are written.

p. 9. Only scribbles.

On the same page of the album are two sets of illuminated letters cut from manuscripts (cent. xiii or xiv). One set consists of a small A–X and three large and finely executed letters, B, C, D, on gold grounds. The other set is a single alphabet, A–U.

On p. 20 is a single large and ably executed A, in red and black, of Cent. xvi. German?

INDEX

In each reference, the first figure, in heavy type, shows the no. of the MS.; the second shows the page.

N.B.—Not every proper name, e.g. of Saints, is included in this index.